COLUMBIA UNIVERSITY
STUDIES IN THE
SOCIAL SCIENCES

92

This Series was formerly known as
Studies in History, Economics and Public Law

THE CONFLICT OVER JUDICIAL POWERS

AMS PRESS
NEW YORK

THE CONFLICT OVER JUDICIAL POWERS

In the United States to 1870

BY

CHARLES GROVE HAINES

AMS PRESS

NEW YORK

The Library of Congress cataloged this title as follows:

Haines, Charles Grove, 1879–1948.
    The conflict over judicial powers in the
United States to 1870. New York, AMS Press
[1970]
    181 p. 23 cm. (Studies in history,
economics, and public law, 92)
    Reprint of the 1909 ed. Includes
bibliographical references.
    ISBN 0-404-510922
    1. Judicial review—United States.   I.
Title.   II. Series: Columbia studies in the
social sciences, 92
KF4575 .H3 1970   71–120213
            347.99/73

Reprinted from the edition of 1909, New York.
First AMS edition published in 1970.
Second AMS printing: 1979

Manufactured in the United States of America.

AMS PRESS INC.
NEW YORK, N.Y.

PREFACE

THIS essay is the outgrowth of a special study of one of the problems of constitutional law begun at Ursinus College in 1903, under the direction of Dr. J. Lynn Barnard, now of the School of Pedagogy, Philadelphia. The main features of the monograph were planned and partially developed while pursuing the courses in constitutional law offered by Professor John W. Burgess, Dean of the Faculty of Political Science of Columbia University. The search has been continued in the reports of judicial decisions, executive messages, legislative debates and resolutions and newspaper comment for public sentiment bearing on the right of the judiciary to declare legislative acts void.

American constitutional history reveals an almost continuous conflict over the assertion of this right by the judiciary in the United States. The controversy originated at the time when the rising nationality in America found itself at the parting of the ways—toward a supreme power in the legislature, or toward a modified form of supremacy in courts of justice. The contest, begun when judges refused to execute legislative acts which they considered contrary to fundamental laws or constitutions, has been one of the foremost problems in the practical working of our federal government, and, according to the recent indications, is likely to assume greater importance in the future.

This study aims to trace the sentiment relative to the exercise of judicial authority prior to 1870. The purpose has been to show the gradual development of the extraordinary powers of the judiciary in the United States, and to present a brief analysis of representative opinions on the conflict involved in this development. The rapid industrial progress since 1870 and the extension of judicial authority resulting therefrom has led to a series of controversies which will require a separate treatment.

Scarcely more than a beginning has been made in the vast field of material which is included within the scope of this paper. In fact, since the sources to be examined cover such a wide range of history, government, politics and law no contribution is likely to offer much of permanent value unless it has been the outgrowth of a life-long study in constitutional history and political practice. With a keen appreciation of the limitations of this attempt, the following pages, offered as a preliminary essay, are intended to serve merely as an introduction to a more exhaustive treatise.

In the preparation of Chapter I, I have been obliged to make constant use of the collection of cases and notes prepared and edited by the late Professor Thayer, in his *Cases on Constitutional Law*, and the essay of Brinton Coxe on *Judicial Power and Unconstitutional Legislation*, edited by William M. Meigs, Esq. For an account of a few of the conflicts of the states with the federal judiciary, the historical notes and papers in the collection of *State Documents on Federal Relations* by Professor H. V. Ames, have been relied upon. I wish, therefore, to express my appreciation for the aid received from these works.

I also wish to acknowledge my indebtedness to Professor Charles A. Beard of Columbia University for sympathetic guidance and the many helpful criticisms, which have made it possible to present the essay in its present form, to Dr. Barnard for valuable suggestions at every step in the preparation of manuscript, and to Professor Burgess for the inspiration toward a critical study of public law in the light of modern historical methods.

CHARLES G. HAINES.

COLLEGEVILLE, PA., MAY 1, 1909.

CONTENTS

CHAPTER V

PRINCIPLES OF THE JACKSONIAN DEMOCRACY

CHAPTER VI

JUDICIAL POWERS FROM 1856 TO 1870.

CHAPTER I

JUDICIAL POWERS BEFORE THE ADOPTION OF THE FEDERAL CONSTITUTION

1. *The Legislature Supreme*

In England. The revolution of 1688 established the supremacy of the legislative department in England. The legislature, it was contended, represented directly the wishes of the people and all other departments of government were ultimately to submit to the legislative will. Blackstone only enunciated a well-recognized maxim of English law when he said that if Parliament, by means of statute or edict made by the king with the advice and consent of the lords and commons, will positively enact a thing to be done which is unreasonable, there is no power to control it, and that " where the main object of a statute is unreasonable the judges are not at liberty to reject it, for that were to set the judicial power above that of the legislature, which would be subversive of all government." [1] John Locke had expressed a similar doctrine in his treatises on government where he said " there can be but one supreme power, which is the legislative, to which all the rest are and must be subordinate, yet the legislative being only a fiduciary power to act for certain ends, there remains still in the people a supreme power to remove or alter the legislative, when they find the legislative act contrary to the trust reposed in

---

[1] Blackstone's *Commentaries* (1st edition), introduction, sec. 3, pp. 85, 91.

them." [1]   Over the people and their direct agents, the legislature, there was to be no controlling force.   A legislative
act with the intent clearly expressed thus could be nullified only by a repeal in the legislature or by a revolution.

According to the popular theories regarding the law of
nature and the contractual basis of government, an absolute,
uncontrollable sovereignty such as that defined by Hobbes [2]
was denied to the government.   Although Locke believed
that the legislative branch must be regarded as supreme
while government exists, he defined certain limitations on
legislative power.   Absolute arbitrary power, governing
without settled standing laws, could not be reconciled with
the ends of society and government.   The law of nature
and the sacred rights of property were not to be interfered
with through legislation.[3]   But no way was suggested by
which legislation could be set aside, except by revolution
when the body of people regarded the cause of sufficient
moment.[4]   Blackstone also recognized that there were laws
so sacred and immutable that they were not to be changed
by legislation.   On account of the fact that all human laws
depend upon the law of nature and the law of revelation, no
enactment should be suffered to contradict these.[5]   He,
however, indicated no method by which these higher laws
could be enforced against the legislative authority.

In America.   When the sovereignty of Great Britain
over the American colonies was thrown off, it was thought
that in the change from colonial dependence to a state of

[1] Locke, *Treatises of government*, ii, chap. xiii, sec. 149.

[2] Thomas Hobbes, *Leviathan*, chaps. xviii, xix.

[3] *Treatises of government*, ii, chap. xi, secs. 136, 137, 138.

[4] *Ibid.*, sec. 68.   Since there is no possibility of an appeal to any
power on earth, Locke thinks that whenever the people have just cause
they are at liberty to appeal to heaven.

[5] Blackstone's *Commentaries*, p. 42.

independence the authority of the British Parliament had been transferred to the legislatures of the colonies. The declarations in the bills of rights of the constitutions of 1776 indicate the general belief in this transfer of power. The constitution of Maryland declared, " that no power of suspending laws, or the execution of laws, unless by or derived from the legislature, ought to be exercised or allowed." [1] That of North Carolina, 1776, affirmed, " that all powers of suspending laws, or the execution of laws, by any authority without consent of the representatives of the people, is injurious to their rights, and ought not to be exercised." [2] Similarly the Massachusetts bill of rights of 1780 provided that, " the power of suspending the laws, or the execution of the laws, ought never to be exercised but by the legislature, or by authority derived from it, to be exercised in such particular cases only as the legislature shall expressly provide for." [3]

There were, however, general provisions that the principles of the constitution were not to be violated. But again no plan was proposed to prevent such violations, except in New York where a council of revision was established for the purpose of examining all laws and of determining whether they were in accord with the constitution, [4]

---

[1] Poore, *Charters and Constitutions,* pt. i, p. 818, art. vii.

[2] *Ibid.,* pt. ii, p. 1409, art. v.

[3] *Ibid.,* pt. i, p. 959, art. xx.

[4] *Ibid.,* pt. ii, p. 1332, art. iii. Maryland enacted " that this declaration of rights, or the form of government, to be established by this convention, or any part or either of them, ought not to be altered, changed or abolished by the legislature of this state, but in such manner as this convention shall prescribe and direct." *Ibid.,* pt. i, p. 820, art. xlii. North Carolina provided " that this declaration of rights . . . ought never to be violated, on any pretense whatsoever." *Ibid.,* pt. ii, p. 1414, art. xliv.

and in Vermont a council of censors was constituted, consisting of thirteen persons elected by the freemen, whose duty it was among other things to enquire whether the constitution had been preserved inviolate in every part.[1]

The ultimate power was supposed to rest with the people, who might overturn any act of their representatives, but this did not interfere with the location of supreme authority in the hands of the legislature. In fact, the legislative department, according to the accepted notions of the time, was the only body in which it was thought supreme power might be located. The people were accustomed to look to their representatives in the house of assembly, as their only protectors against arbitrary action. The legislature frequently interfered with the judiciary department. They passed acts vacating and annulling judgments. They often constituted themselves courts of chancery. The powers thus exercised with the approbation of a majority of the people, naturally confirmed the idea that the legislature was unlimited and supreme. " No idea was entertained," said a Vermont lawyer in 1824 " that the judiciary had any power to inquire into the constitutionality of acts of the legislature, or to pronounce them void for any cause, or even to question their validity." [2] Long after 1785 the power of the courts to pass on the constitutionality of laws was held to be " anti-republican."

Madison's Opinion. The tendency toward legislative supremacy came up in the discussion over the principle of the separation of powers while the federal Constitution was

---

[1] I D. Chipman, *Vermont Reports*, 20.

[2] I D. Chipman's *Reports*, 13, 22, *et seq.* See also Swift, *System of the Laws of Connecticut*, published in 1795, wherein the author argues that " it is as probable that the judiciary will declare laws unconstitutional which are not so as it is that the legislature will exceed their constitutional authority." Vol. i, p. 50.

being drafted. Madison expressed fears regarding the development toward supreme legislative power in the states. " The legislative department," he remarked, " is everywhere extending the sphere of its activity, and drawing all power into its impetuous vortex." [1] The founders of our republic " seem never to have recollected the danger from legislative usurpations, which, by assembling all power in the same hands, must lead to the same tyranny as is threatened by executive usurpation." [2] It was the opinion of Madison that any project of usurpation by either the executive or the judiciary would immediately be defeated since the legislative department would necessarily hold the controlling power. There was no doubt in his mind that legislative authority ought to be restricted, but the means of security against this authority was a great problem to be solved. In his judgment the people ought to indulge all their jealousy and exhaust all their precaution against the enterprising ambition of the legislative department. But, he observed, " it is not possible to give to each department an equal power 'of self-defense. In republican government, the legislative authority necessarily predominates." [3]

The remedy against legislative usurpation was provided for in the division of the legislature into two branches with a veto in the hands of the executive. [4] It was taken for granted that the legislature would have the upper hand. Both the executive veto and judicial review, so far as it was admitted, were intended primarily to prevent the exercise of judicial and executive functions by the legislature. A manifest intrusion into the realm of either of the other departments was to be resisted, but ultimately on all the

[1] *The Federalist* (Ford's Edition), no. xlviii, p. 328.

[2] *Ibid.*, p. 328.

[3] *The Federalist*, no. li, p. 345.   [4] *Ibid.*, no. li.

great issues of government the legislative department was to have controlling force.

If the principle of legislative supremacy in England and in the colonies was so well under way by 1776, how did the courts secure the right to refuse to enforce a legislative act? The origin of this practice of American constitutional law is to be found in a precedent established in a few English cases, prior to the revolution of 1688, in the arguments of colonial cases, in the practice of several state courts immediately following the revolution, in the debates in the Philadelphia convention regarding the federal judiciary and in the opinion of Hamilton in *The Federalist*.

2. *Restrictions on Legislative Authority in England.*

Transfer of sovereignty. During the reign of the Stuarts in England the exact location of sovereignty or the supreme power of the state was in process of transition. It was not clearly understood that sovereignty, the ultimate power in the state could not be limited. When the supreme power was alternately claimed by an absolute executive and a legislature inclined to become equally absolute, inconsistencies were likely to arise. The fundamental maxim by which nothing was to be counted law which was contrary to the law of God or the law of reason, so potent and useful against the arbitrary acts of a divine-right king, was similarly applied to the exercise of legislative authority. Blackstone, as has been seen,[1] tried to reconcile two political principles which appear contradictory in the light of modern political theory. If acts of parliament contrary to reason were void then the authority which could declare them so would have been the supreme power in the state. Two principles were in apparent conflict, one that Parliament

---

[1] *Cf. supra*, pp. 11-12.

was limited, the other that Parliament was unlimited. While England has worked steadily in the direction of the latter position, our government has laid its foundation in the policy indicated by the former. It is necessary, therefore, to examine the method by which Parliament was to be limited and to note the first restrictions placed upon the legislative authority in the colonies.

Denial of sovereignty of Parliament. In the report of decisions by Chief Justice Hobart, published in 1641, a case is cited wherein it is indicated that acts of Parliament will not be executed if found to be contrary to natural justice. An action of trespass raised a question regarding the procedure to be followed in a trial. According to the opinion of Justice Hobart, the fact that the procedure in the case was confirmed by act of Parliament was immaterial, both because the act could not have intended such a result and because " even an act of Parliament made against natural equity as to make a man judge in his own case, is void in itself." [1] A more direct opinion was rendered in Dr. Bonham's case wherein an imprisonment for the illegal practice of medicine was not upheld, regardless of the fact that certain acts of Parliament sanctioned the imprisonment. The decision was practically based upon the contention " that in many cases the common law will control acts of Parliament, and sometimes adjudge them to be utterly void, for when an act of Parliament is against common right and reason, or repugnant, or impossible to be performed, the common law will control it, and adjudge such acts to be void." [2] A few years later Chief Justice Coke is reported to have said

[1] Hobart's *Reports,* Common Pleas, 120.
[2] *Reports* of Sir Edward Coke, iv, 234.

That Fortesque and Littleton, and all others agreed that the common law consists of three parts: first, common law; secondly, statute law, which corrects, abridges, and explains the common law; the third, custom, which takes away the common law. But the common law corrects, allows and disallows, both statute law and custom, for if there be repugnancy in statute or unreasonableness in custom, the common law disallows and rejects it.[1]

In an edition of Coke's Littleton, published a few years before the meeting of the Philadelphia convention, the editor maintained that " the surest construction of a statute, is by the rule and reason of the common law." [2]   An instance was cited in which the judges for the " advancement and expedition " of justice extended a statute against the letter of the law.   The courts as the interpreters and expounders of the common law were to be superior to Parliament, in that they could set aside the well-formulated will of the highest legislative assembly in the realm.   This principle was asserted by the judges before the revolution of 1688, was regularly repeated in the law texts of the middle of the eighteenth century, and appears to have been cited in arguments almost to the time of the outbreak of the American Revolution.   Blackstone deemed it necessary to state the principle of judicial control of legislative acts,[3] even though he found it necessary to contradict the prin-

[1] *Reports* collected by Richard Brownlow, p. 652, Rowles *vs.* Mason, 197, 198.

[2] Coke's *Littleton* (revised edition), sec. 464.

[3] In his later editions the instances where courts may interfere with the will of Parliament are greatly restricted by narrowing the principle of the earlier cases to acts that are impossible to be performed or acts wherein absurd consequences may arise. In such instances the courts may prevent legislative errors. Sharswood, Blackstone's *Commentaries,* p. 90.

ciple as a result of the practice which had been growing in favor of an unlimited Parliament.

3. *Judicial resistance to Legislative Acts in America.*

The colonies founded on American soil were organized under the supremacy of the English government. Colonial authorities were limited by charters or other instruments of government, and were subject to the superior power of the Crown and the British Parliament. Colonial laws had to be in harmony with the laws of the realm, and if found to be repugnant could be set aside as null and void. Generally appeals could be taken from the colonial courts to the assemblies and thence to the privy council. In the case of Winthrop *vs.* Lechmere,[1] and in other instances, colonial statutes were declared void on account of their repugnance to the charter and the English law. Though such cases of judicial nullification of colonial statutes were rare, nevertheless the idea of a supreme court of justice which could set aside acts of colonial assemblies was clearly impressed upon the colonists.

Argument of James Otis. In the famous controversy over the Writs of Assistance, Otis denied the right of Parliament to determine ultimately the validity of its own acts. " Reason and the constitution," he argued, " are both against this writ . . . No acts of Parliament can establish such a writ; though it should be made in the very words of the petition, it would be void. An act against the constitution is void." [2] The prevailing reason given as the

---

[1] 5 Massachusetts Historical Society Collection (sixth series), p. 440. See 4 Connecticut Historical Society Collection, p. 94, for an account of the cases—Phillips *vs.* Savage, 1734, and Clark *vs.* Tousby, 1745.

[2] *John Adams, Works,* edited by Charles Francis Adams, vol. ii, appendix. p. 525.

basis of resistance, was that the Stamp Act was against *Magna Charta* and the natural rights of Englishmen and therefore null and void.[1] The views of Lord Coke and Chief Justice Hobart were applied to this American case at a time when the principle on which the English cases were based had been discarded in England in favor of a complete sovereignty in Parliament. It was of little moment that the argument of Otis was not in accordance with the existing law of England: it suited the aim and purpose of the colonists, in resisting the claims of a Parliament which in their judgment was arbitrarily legislating against them; it furnished a plausible theory for the right of resistance, which developed rapidly into open rebellion.

Fear of absolute authority in the government. When legislative supremacy noted above [2] was on a fair way to be established in all of the colonies, a contrary principle was announced in several state courts which led to a very different development. Unlimited power in government came to be regarded as a danger greatly to be feared. The legislature was to be restricted, but in such a manner as to leave it free for all useful purposes. The colonists thought they had been humiliated as a result of the omnipotent power of the British Parliament. " We felt in all its rigor," said Justice Iredell, " the mischiefs of an absolute and unbounded authority, claimed by so weak a creature as man, and should have been guilty of the basest breach of trust, as well as the grossest folly, if in the same moment when we spurned the insolent depotism of Great Britain, we had established a despotic power ourselves." [3] It was feared that governments were inclined to develop toward absolu-

---

[1] *John Adams, op. cit.,* vol. i, pp. 158, 159.

[2] *Cf. supra,* pp. 12-14.

[3] G. J. McRee, *Life and Correspondence of James Iredell,* ii, p. 146.

tism. Individuals were likely to suffer an infringement of personal liberty or property rights unless definite barriers were interposed. Conservative leaders thought that political power was of an encroaching nature, and that it ought to be effectually restrained from passing the limits assigned to it. The chief criticism of the draft of the federal Constitution was the absence of a bill of rights to safeguard individual liberty.[1]

The principle applied in a few rather unimportant cases in England before the revolution of 1688, and relied upon in the defence by Otis before the colonial court in Massachusetts, was brought forth to put a check upon the tendency toward legislative dominance and to preserve the inviolability of written constitutions. The executive was not to be feared, for the people held a sufficient power over him; but the private rights of the individual, which loomed up so significantly in the eighteenth-century political philosophy, were to be protected from the encroachments of an overzealous legislature. The rights of the minority were to be made secure against what might become an arbitrary rule of the majority. Therefore in direct contradiction to the principle of legislative supremacy, firmly established in England by the revolution of 1688, the state courts adopted the principle that a law contrary to the constitution or contrary to the principles of natural law and justice was void, and that it was the duty of the courts to restrain the legislative authority by refusing to execute such a law.

Holmes vs. Walton. The courts of New Jersey seem to have led the way in asserting the principle of a judicial con-

---

[1] The arguments of those opposed to the adoption of the Constitution are filled with fears of such encroachments. See *Pamphlets on the Constitution, 1787-8,* Ford, particularly, *Observations on the New Constitution,* by Elbridge Gerry, pp. 6, 12.

trol over legislation, in the case of Holmes *vs.* Walton, decided in the year 1780. The case was brought before the Supreme Court of the state in September, 1779 and was argued on constitutional grounds.[1] In the enforcement of the state seizure laws it was enacted that the trial should be by a jury of six men. The point was raised that this was not a constitutional jury.[2] The court considered the question at three sessions and finally on September 7th, 1780, the statute was held to be unconstitutional and inoperative. As a result of the attitude of the court it is claimed that the part of the act which related to the six-men jury was repealed and a jury of twelve men substituted.[3] No authentic report of the case has been preserved and little is known regarding the manner in which the decision of the court was received. Gouverneur Morris, in a reference to this decision in 1785, remarked, " they know that the boasted omnipotence of legislative authority is but a jingle of words. In the literal meaning it is impious. And whatever interpretation lawyers may give, freemen must feel it to be absurd and unconstitutional. Absurd, because laws cannot alter the nature of things; unconstitutional, because the constitution is no more, if it can be changed by the legislature."[4] In New Jersey, he notes, the judges have pronounced a law unconstitutional and void; but he did not wish to see the courts of Pennsylvania decide upon the constitutionality of acts for fear that such power in the hands of judges would be dangerous. Morris thought, however, that such a power ought to exist some-

---

[1] Austin Scott, 2 American Historical Papers, pp. 45-47.

[2] State *vs.* Parkhurst, 9 New Jersey, 549, cited in the opinion of Chief Justice Kirkpatrick.

[3] *Ibid.,* p. 549, Laws of New Jersey (first edition), p. 49.

[4] Sparks, *Life of Gouverneur Morris,* iii, p. 438.

where to maintain the fundamental provisions of government.

Commonwealth vs. Caton. In Virginia, two years later, the case of Commonwealth *vs.* Caton [1] raised the question whether the courts could declare void an act of assembly. Justice Wythe fearlessly maintained that, as a member of the court, it was plainly and unmistakably his duty to resist the legislature in an attempted exercise of powers inconsistent with the constitution, and observed that, " if the whole legislature . . . should attempt to overleap the bounds prescribed to them by the people, I, in administering the public justice of the country, will meet the united powers at my seat in this tribunal; and pointing to the constitution will say to them here is the limit of your authority, and hither shall you go but no further." [2]

Justice Pendleton raised the query:

How far this court, in whom the judiciary powers may in some sort be said to be concentrated, shall have power to declare the nullity of a law passed in its forms by the legislative power, without exercising the power of that branch, contrary to the plain terms of that constitution, is indeed a deep, im-

---

[1] John Caton, Joshua Hopkins, and John Lamb were condemned for treason by the General Court under the act of assembly concerning that offense, passed in 1776, which took from the executive the power of granting pardon in such cases. The house of delegates by resolution of 18th of June, 1782, granted them a pardon, and sent it to the senate for concurrence, which they refused. The men continued in jail under the sentence until in October, 1782, when the attorney general moved in the General Court, that execution of judgment might be awarded. The prisoners pleaded the pardon granted by the house of delegates. The attorney general denied the validity of the pardon as the senate had not concurred in it, and the General Court adjourned the case, for novelty and difficulty, to the Court of Appeals. The court held the pardon invalid because the senate had not concurred in the resolution. 4 Call, *Virginia Reports*, 5.

[2] 4 Call, 8.

portant, and I will add, a tremendous question, the decisions of which might involve consequences to which gentlemen may not have extended their ideas.[1]

He did not think this question was actually at issue in the case. The court gave as its opinion that it had the power to declare acts of the legislature unconstitutional and void,[2] but as the senate had not concurred in the resolution which was under consideration, and as a consequence no regular statute was before the court the decision did not serve as a very strong precedent.

Rutgers vs. Waddington. Determined opposition to the assertion of this right by a court of justice did not appear until the judgment was announced in the case of Rutgers *vs.* Waddington [3] in 1784. An action of trespass against Joshua Waddington brought up for consideration an act of the legislature of New York.[4] After having stated the rule of Blackstone and affirmed the doctrine, "that the su-

---

[1] 4 Call, 17.   [2] *Ibid.,* 20.

[3] The case arose out of an action for trespass brought against Joshua Waddington for the occupation of a brewery belonging to Elizabeth Rutgers, during part of the period covered by the Revolutionary War, 1778 to 1783. The action arose under a statute of New York which provided that where by reason of the invasion of the enemy anyone who left his place of abode, who had not voluntarily put himself into the power of the enemy should be entitled to recover in an action of trespass against any person or persons, who may have occupied or destroyed his estate. It developed in the trial, that from Sept., 1778 to April, 1780, the premises had been occupied by order of the military commander in charge of the district and that the actual voluntary trespass covered from April, 1780 to March, 1783, the date of the passage of the above act. The court felt at liberty to disregard the direct terms of the act and awarded damages only for the latter period, claiming that it could not have been the intention of the legislature to work such a manifest hardship upon the defendant as would result from a literal interpretation of the statute.

[4] Act Sessions Laws, March 17th, 1783 (original edition), pp. 283, 284.

premacy of the legislature need not be called into question,"
the court proceeded to disregard that part of the statute
which would, as it seemed, operate unreasonably. A decision was rendered to the effect that although a statute
must be regarded as obligatory, collateral matters which
arise out of the general words which happen to be unreasonable may be disregarded by the court.[1]

The " violent Whigs," as those were called who belonged
to Clinton's party, considered the decision " subversive of
good order and the sovereignty of the state; " and, on the
13th of September, 1784, a meeting was called to discuss
ways and means of bringing the dangers of the decision
before the public. As a result of this meeting a committee
was appointed to prepare and publish an address to the
people of the state.[2] The history and facts of the case
are briefly stated and an elaborate criticism rendered, the
main features of which are as follows: From the statement of the case as given, it appeared to the committee
that the Mayor's Court had assumed and exercised a power
to set aside an act of the state; that it had permitted the
vague and doubtful custom of nations to be placed against,
and to render abortive, a clear and positive statute.

This proceeding, in the opinion of a great part of the citizens
of this metropolis, and in our opinion, is an assumption of
power in that court, which is inconsistent with the nature and
genius of our government, and threatening to the liberties of
the people.[3]

[1] *An Account of the Case of Elizabeth Rutgers vs. Joshua Waddington* was prepared and edited with an historical introduction by Henry
B. Dawson; see p. 41.

[2] Davis, *Memoirs of Aaron Burr*, ii, p. 45. The address was published in the New York *Packet*, and the *American Advertiser*, no.
434, Thursday, November 4th, 1784. See Dawson's *Pamphlet*, pp. 25-40.

[3] Dawson, *Historical Introduction, op. cit.*, pp. 29, 33.

From what has been said, we think that no one can doubt the meaning of the law. It remains to inquire whether a court of Judicature can, consistently with our Constitution and laws, adjudicate contrary to the plain and obvious meaning of a statute. That the Mayor's Court has done so in this case we think is manifest from the aforegoing remarks. That there should be a power vested in courts of judicature, whereby they might control the supreme legislative power, we think is absurd in itself. Such power in courts would be destructive of liberty, and remove all security of property. The design of courts of justice, in our government from the very nature of their institution, is to declare laws, not to alter them. Whenever they depart from this design of their institution, they confound legislative and judicial powers.[1]

Now the reasoning of the court and the reasoning of the legislature may lead them to very different conclusions. And as the court reasons last upon the case, it is utterly impossible for any man to guess the result, when he brings a suit, however exactly the law may apply to the case, until through a tedious and expensive process he obtains the opinion of the court.[2] The arrangements for an independent judiciary are regarded as necessary and essential when judges keep within their proper sphere.

But if they [the judges] are to be invested with a power to overrule a plain law, . . . [if] they may judge the law unreasonable, because not consonant to the law of nations or to the opinion of ancient or modern civilians and philosophers, for whom they may have a greater veneration than for the solid statutes and supreme legislative power of the state,—we say, if they are to assume and exercise such a power, the probable consequences of their independence will be the most deplorable. That the laws should be no longer absolute would

[1] Dawson, *op. cit.*, pp. 33, 34.   [2] *Ibid.*, p. 34.

be in itself a great evil, but a far more dreadful consequence arises . . . [since] power is not lost in the controversy, but transferred to judges who are independent of the people.[1]

The principle of the case was denounced as dangerous to the freedom of our government, and the committee believed that a perseverance in that principle would leave our legislatures nothing but a name. The address was closed by calling attention to the fact that the acceptance of such a doctrine would lead to a revolution in government.[2]

On October 27th, 1784, on motion of Mr. Harper, a resolution was introduced in the assembly with a recommendation to appoint such persons to the offices of mayor and recorder of New York City " as will govern themselves by the known laws of the land." [3] Although this motion was rejected the house passed a vote of censure on the court, as follows: " Resolved that the judgment aforesaid is, in its tendency, subversive of all law and good order and leads directly to anarchy and confusion; because if a court instituted for the benefit and government of a corporation may take upon them to dispense with, and act in direct violation of, a plain and known law of the state, all other courts, either superior or inferior, may do the like; and therewith will end all our dear bought rights and privileges, and legislatures become useless." [4] The case was soon compromised and a serious conflict between the two departments of government was averted.[5]

---

[1] Dawson, *op. cit.,* p. 36.

[2] *Ibid.,* pp. 39, 40.

[3] Journal of Assembly, pp. 22-29.

[4] *Ibid.,* pp. 32-34.

[5] Alexander Hamilton, referring to the decision remarked: " even the suit of Rutgers *vs.* Waddington, after a partial success in the

Trevett vs. Weeden. The case which came before the supreme court of Rhode Island in 1786, is one of the landmarks in the establishment of judicial authority in the United States.[1]   An act of assembly relating to the acceptance of bank bills as specie was made enforcible through a summary conviction without a jury trial. The act was thought to be at variance with the colonial charter which served as the constitution of the state. The supreme court refused to carry out the plain intention of the legislature by declining to take jurisdiction of the complaint presented in accordance with the act.[2]   On account of this decision the two houses of assembly joined in a resolution, as follows:

Whereas it appears that the honorable judges of the supreme court of judicature, at the last September term of said court in the county of Newport, have by the judgment of said court, adjudged an act of the supreme legislature of this state to be unconstitutional and so absolutely void; and whereas it is suggested that the said judgment is unprecedented in this state

Mayor's Court, was terminated by a compromise, according to the advice of defendant's council, owing to the apprehension of an unfavorable issue in the supreme court; and this, notwithstanding the defendant was a British subject." Lodge, *The Works of Alexander Hamilton*, vol. v, p. 227.

1 This was an information against John Weeden for refusing to receive the paper bills of the state, as an equivalent for silver or gold, in payment for meat sold in the market. By a special act of assembly the penalty of such refusal was fixed at one hundred pounds and the court was to proceed to trial without any jury toward an immediate sentence from which there was to be no appeal. After due consideration the court delivered a unanimous opinion that the information was not cognizable before them, suggesting that the penal law was unjust and unconstitutional.

2 Owing to the fact that the pamphlet by James M. Varnum dealing with this case was not accessible, I have relied upon the report of it as given by J. B. Thayer in his *Cases on Constitutional Law*, vol. i, pp. 73-78.

and may tend to abolish the legislative authority thereof: it is therefore voted and resolved that all the justices of said court be forthwith cited by the sheriffs of the respective counties in which they live or may be found, to give their immediate attendance upon this assembly, to assign the reasons and grounds for the aforesaid judgment and that the clerk of said court be directed to attend this assembly at the same time with the records of the court which relate to the said judgment.[1]

One of the judges in his remarks before the assembly maintained that " for the reason of their judgments upon any question judicially before them, they [the judges] were accountable only to God and their own consciences." [2] The assembly was not satisfied with the answers and a motion was made for dismissal from office. As the judges of the state could be removed by law only as a result of preferred charges in a regular trial, the motion was lost, but at the next annual election by the legislature four of the justices who gave the adverse decision, excepting only the Chief Justice, were dropped and others favorable to the wishes of the assembly were appointed.[3] Before the new judges took their seats the obnoxious law was repealed, and the courts had gained a partial victory which was not readily forgotten. As was the rule in almost every one of the early cases, public sentiment seems to have supported the contention of the court and the legislature was obliged to submit, however much the bold assumptions of the judges might be condemned.

Prior to the meeting of the Philadelphia convention judicial authority had been asserted and maintained above

[1] *Acts and Resolves,* R. I., October, 1786, p. 6.

[2] Thayer, *op. cit.,* p. 76.

[3] 2 Chandler's *Criminal Trials,* p. 269. See also Brinton Coxe, *Judicial Power and Unconstitutional Legislation,* for an account of this case.

the will of the legislature in three states, New Jersey, New York and Rhode Island. In two instances definite provisions in legislative acts had been nullified through judicial determinations. In three cases, Holmes *vs.* Walton, an unreported case in Massachusetts [1] and Trevett *vs.* Weeden, the laws to which objections were raised were repealed by the legislature, which is evidence of the general impression regarding the supremacy of the legislature and the belief that the judiciary could not of its own will set aside a legislative act. The courts might raise objections and render criticisms; the legislature alone was competent to remove the legal effects of the act.

Den vs. Singleton. While the convention was in session a case was brought before the court in North Carolina, which attracted much attention.[2] It was the first case in

[1] On July 11th, 1788, J. B. Cutting wrote to Jefferson commenting upon what he termed " the manly proceeding of a Virginia court of appeals." " I may venture to applaud," he continues, " the integrity of judges who thus fulfil their oaths and their duties. I am proud of such characters." He informed Jefferson that an act of legislature was declared unconstitutional by the supreme court of Massachusetts, and stated that at the very next session of the legislature the law was formally repealed, although he doubted the necessity of such a procedure. Bancroft, *History of the Constitution of the United States,* vol. ii, pp. 472, 473. For an article on this case concerning which there seems to be much doubt, see 7 *Harvard Law Review,* " An Early Constitutional Case in Massachusetts," by A. C. Goodell, Jr.

[2] 1 Martin, North Carolina *Reports,* 42. This was an action for the recovery of a house and lot under an act to secure in their possession all persons who had purchased lands sold by commissioners of forfeited estates. The act required the court " in all cases where the defendant makes affidavit that he holds the disputed property under a sale from a commissioner of forfeited estates to dismiss the suit on motion." The court refused to follow the act and advised the parties to consent to a fair decision on the property in question by a jury, according to the common law of the land. The act of assembly was thus denied its force and effect because " by the constitution every citizen had undoubtedly a right to a decision of his property by a jury trial."

which there was a conflict between a provision of a regularly adopted written constitution and a legislative act. The court after a reasonable endeavor to avoid disagreement between the legislature and the judicial powers of the state, "with much apparent reluctance, but with great deliberation and firmness gave their opinion separately, but unanimously," against the act under consideration. The judges observed, that the obligation of their oaths and the duty of their office required them to give their opinion on that important and momentous question.[1] The judges thought

It was clear that no act they (the legislature) could pass could by any means repeal or alter the constitution, because if they could do this, they would at the same instant of time dissolve the government thereby established. Consequently the constitution (which the judicial power was bound to take notice of as much as of any other law whatever,) standing in full force as the fundamental law of the land, notwithstanding the act on which the present motion was grounded, the same act must of course, in that instance stand as abrogated and without any effect.[2]

Richard Spaight, who afterwards became governor of the state, wrote to James Iredell, a counsel in the case and a member of the Philadelphia convention, for his opinion regarding the decision. Iredell, who was interested in having a decision favorable to this form of judicial authority, wrote several letters which express very fully the theory on which the earliest instances of interference with legislation were based. His opinion is important as an expression of the sentiment which made judicial nullification of legislative acts possible in America. He considered the constitution

[1] 1 Martin, North Carolina *Reports*, p. 44.
[2] 1 Martin, *op. cit.*, p. 45.

of the state the fundamental basis of government, unalterable except by the same power that established it. " I have therefore no doubt, but that the power of the assembly is limited and defined by the constitution. It is a creature of the constitution." [1] He believed that the judges could not consistently with their duties, carry into effect a law violating the constitution.[2] The constitution limited the power of the legislature and it was the plain and apparent duty of the court to prevent the legislature from overstepping the prescribed limits. Individual rights, he maintained, must be protected by the courts; and above all, the will of the majority must be restrained in the interest of the privileges and liberties of the minority.[3] The rule of the majority was inclined to be inconsiderate of the rights of the individual. Private rights of person and property must be protected at all hazards. " Every citizen should have a surer pledge for his constitutional rights than the wisdom and activity of any occasional majority of his fellow citizens." [4] Courts alone were in a position to protect the individual and to thwart the ultimate rule of the majority. It was therefore incumbent upon them to hold the legislative power in check within the prescribed limits of the constitution as they understood them. The power of the judges is regarded as alarming, since there is no appeal from their jurisdiction; but, as between oppression by legislatures and oppression by the courts, the latter is preferable.

The opposition to the decision was general throughout

[1] McCree, *Life and Correspondence of James Iredell*, vol. ii, pp. 145-146.

[2] *Ibid.*, p. 148.

[3] *Ibid.*, pp. 172-173.

[4] *Ibid.*, p. 176.

the state.   Spaight voiced a very common sentiment in his letter to Iredell.[1]   He writes:

I do not pretend to vindicate the law which has been the subject of controversy; it is immaterial what law they have declared void; it is their usurpation of the authority to do it, that I complain of, as I do most positively deny that they have any such power; nor can they find anything in the constitution either directly or impliedly, that will support them, or give them any color of right to exercise that authority.   Besides, it would have been absurd, and contrary to the practice of all the world, had the constitution vested such power in them, as they would have operated as an absolute negative on the proceedings of the legislature, which no judiciary ought ever to possess, and the state, instead of being governed by the representatives in the general assembly would be subject to the will of three individuals, who united in their own persons the legislative and judiciary powers, which no monarch in Europe enjoys, and which would be more despotic than the Roman decemvirate, and equally insufferable.[2]

Spaight expressed the belief which was almost universally held at the time that the legislative authority ought to be restricted, but he could see no way to effect this except by the exercise of suffrage at the polls.   In this manner, he thought, a legislative act contrary to the constitution and the natural principles of justice could be effectually annulled. According to Iredell the great argument of those in opposition was that "though the assembly have no right to violate the constitution, yet if they do so, the only remedy is either by an humble petition that the law may be repealed, or a universal resistance of the people.   In the meantime

---

[1] See 103 N. C. Reports, "History of the Supreme Court of North Carolina," by Hon. Kemp P. Battle, pp. 472, 473.

[2] McCree, *op. cit.*, pp. 169, 170.

their act, whatever it is, is to be obeyed as a law; for the judicial power is not to presume to question the power of an act of assembly." [1]

Committee on Appeals in Congress. After a number of cases arising out of conflicts over the law of nations had been brought on appeal from the individual states to Congress, a committee was appointed on January 30th, 1777, whose duty it was to determine upon cases of capture of prizes at sea and other cases arising under international relations.[2] This committee was superseded in January, 1780, by a court of appeals which continued to hear cases until the final adjournment of the court in 1787.[3] The decisions of these federal tribunals were generally acceptable, and the narrow realm covered by the Committee of Appeals led to the settlement of some difficult controversies growing out of the Revolutionary War. The decision of the Court of Appeals in the case of the Sloop Active was flagrantly disregarded by the authorities of Pennsylvania, with the result that the court lost much of the little power it formerly possessed. It was this tribunal, no doubt, which furnished a model for the Supreme Court of the United States.

In April, 1787, the Congress of the Confederation passed a significant resolution indicating the trend of affairs relative to the confidence in judicial authority. The question came up for consideration regarding the repeal of state laws contrary to the provisions of the treaty of peace. Congress enacted that any acts or parts of acts repugnant to the treaty of peace were thereby repealed, and that the courts of law were to decide and adjudge anything in said acts contrary to the treaty as void.[4] It was the opinion of

[1] McCree, *op. cit.*, p. 146.
[2] *Journals of Congress*, iii, p. 34.   [3] *Ibid.*, vi, p. 10.
[4] *Journals of Congress* (edition 1801), vol. xii, p. 35.

Congress that " by repealing in general terms all acts and clauses repugnant to the treaty, the business will be turned over to its proper department viz., the judicial; and the courts of law will find no difficulty in deciding whether any particular act or clause is or is not contrary to the treaty." [1] Prior to the above date, judicial authority was exercised almost entirely by state courts. Supreme courts or final tribunals of appeal were organized by Congress, but in extreme cases the ultimate decision of a controversy rested with the state legislature if that body did not act in sole capacity as a court of errors. [2]

The political theories of the time favored judicial restriction of state laws to the point of practical nullification. The same trend of thought regarded the federal courts as the only proper tribunals to determine the validity or the invalidity of state laws contrary to the terms of the treaty of peace or to the principles of the law of nations. In practice a principle was emerging, not sanctioned by any positive enactment, which dealt a severe blow to the power of the legislative department. State courts were asserting authority above that of the legislative assemblies. Federal courts were claiming the right to declare void state laws contrary to national laws and treaties, and contrary to the "sovereign rights of peace and war" vested in the Confederate Congress. It was but a short step, therefore, to Marbury *vs.* Madison.

---

[1] *Journals of Congress* (edition 1801), vol. xii, p. 36.

[2] In New Jersey as well as in New York the final judicial authority was a branch of the legislature. *The Federalist*, no. xlvi, p. 441; *cf. supra*, pp. 13, 14.

CHAPTER II

EARLY CONFLICTS OVER JUDICIAL NULLIFICATION BY FEDERAL COURTS

1. Judicial authority and the Constitution

Sentiment in the Convention. The sentiment on the functions of the judiciary appears to have been divided in the Constitutional Convention and the few opinions expressed seem to show a lack of careful consideration of the intricate problems involved. A resolution was presented by Edmund Randolph on Tuesday, May 29th, 1787, to the effect that the President and certain members of the national judiciary should have the powers of a council of revision, similar to the plan which had been adopted in New York, with the authority to examine every act of the national legislature, before it should go into operation and also every act of each state legislature before a negative thereon should be final.[1] This resolution was twice voted down by a substantial majority, and the power of examination of congressional acts was given to the President with the proviso that a two-thirds majority in both houses could overrule the executive veto.[2] Martin, Gerry, Mason and Madison seem to have favored placing the revisory authority over federal statutes with the courts.[3] In discussing the weakness of the judicial department in contrast with the legislature, Gerry thought that the courts would have " a suffi-

[1] *Elliot's Debates*, vol. v, p. 128. [2] *Ibid.,* pp. 151, 155.
[3] *Ibid.,* pp. 151, 344, 345.

cient check against encroachments on their own department
by their exposition of the laws, which involved a power of
deciding on their constitutionality.   In some states the
judges had actually set aside the laws as being against the
constitution.   This was done, too, with general approbation." [1]   On the other hand, Pinckney, Mercer and Dickinson were inclined to regard the exercise of this authority
by the courts with disfavor.   Pinckney opposed the interference of the judges in legislative business.   Mercer stated
the axiom that the judiciary ought to be separate from the
legislature and disapproved the doctrine that the judges, as
expositors of the Constitution, should have authority to declare a law void.   He thought laws ought to be well and
cautiously made, and then to be uncontrollable by any other
body. [2]   Dickinson was impressed by the remarks of Mercer,
and thought that the judges ought to exercise no such
power.   The judiciary of Aragon, he remarked, became
by degrees the lawgiver. [3]   What would be regarded to-day
as one of the most significant questions that confronted the
Constitutional Convention was, however, left unsettled.
The whole issue was either intentionally or unintentionally
left open for future solution.

Although no express power to interfere with legislative
acts was given in the provisions of the federal Constitution,
various objections were raised by those who disapproved of
the indefinite language in the articles relating to the judiciary.   In many of the public addresses and papers of the
time the plan of the federal judiciary is severely attacked.
Elbridge Gerry feared that a Star Chamber was about to
be established.   He urged that " there are no well defined

[1] *Elliot's Debates*, vol. v, p. 151.   [2] *Ibid.*, p. 429.

[3] *Ibid.*, p. 429.

limits of the judiciary powers, they seem to be left as a boundless ocean, that has broken over the chart of the Supreme Lawgiver, ' Thus far thou shalt go and no further,' and as they cannot be comprehended by the clearest capacity or the most sagacious mind, it would be a Herculean labor to attempt to describe the dangers with which they are replete." [1]   Edmund Randolph and George Mason, who with Gerry refused to sign the completed document, objected seriously to the fact that there were no limitations to the judicial power.[2]   Mason was alarmed in that he believed the federal judiciary to be so constructed and extended as to absorb and destroy the judiciaries of the several states.[3]   Similar objections were raised by Richard Henry Lee in his letters of a Federal Farmer.[4]

Hamilton's Opinion.   The most exhaustive discussion of the powers of the federal judiciary is to be found in the papers of the Federalist.   In the Philadelphia Convention, Madison thought that the courts might resist legislative encroachments, but in the papers prepared to defend the Constitution he does not deal with this doctrine.   But Hamilton treats very fully of the theory that was accepted by a few of the state courts in the nullification of legislative acts.   In the seventy-eighth number of the Federalist he discusses the powers of the judicial department according to the provisions of the new Constitution.   He first argues that the judiciary will be the weakest of the three departments of the federal government and therefore least likely to usurp power, because it has no influence over the sword or purse, can take no active resolution and must ultimately depend upon the executive for the execution of its judg-

[1] Ford, *Pamphlets on the Constitution*, p. 9.   [2] *Ibid.*, p. 275.
[3] *Ibid.*, pp. 329, 330.   [4] *Ibid.*, pp. 298 *et seq.*

ments.[1] It follows that the liberty of the individual has nothing to fear from this department, but rather that every precaution must be taken by the people that the judiciary is not overawed by the co-ordinate branches of the government.

Very soon, however, he comes directly to the real point at issue and gives an opinion that is unquestionably definite and certain enough to form the basis for all future formulations of the theory underlying the practice of judicial nullification. His argument runs as follows:

The complete independence of the courts of justice is peculiarly essential in a limited constitution. By a limited constitution, I understand one which contains certain specified exceptions to the legislative authority; such, for instance, as that it will pass no bills of attainder, no *ex post facto* laws, and the like. Limitations of this kind can be preserved in practice in no other way than through the medium of the courts of justice, whose duty it must be to declare all acts contrary to the manifest tenor of the Constitution void. Without this, all reservations of particular rights or privileges would amount to nothing.[2]

Because there had been much opposition to the assertion of the right of the courts to pronounce legislative acts void, on the ground that such a right implied a superiority of the judiciary over the legislature, Hamilton felt obliged to vindicate his position with an extended argument:

There is no position which depends on clearer principles than that every act of a delegated authority, contrary to the tenor of the commission under which it is exercised, is void. No

---

[1] *The Federalist* (Ford's edition), no, lxxviii, pp. 518, 519.
[2] *Ibid.*, p. 520.

legislative act, therefore, contrary to the Constitution, can be valid. To deny this would be to affirm that the deputy is greater than his principle; that the servant is above his master; that the representatives of the people are superior to the people themselves; that men acting by virtue of powers, may do not only what their powers do not authorize, but what they forbid.

To the argument that the legislature must be the constitutional judge of its own powers and that the other departments must submit to the construction placed upon the Constitution by the legislature, Hamilton replied that this cannot be because it is not to be found in the provisions of the Constitution. " It is far more rational to suppose," he continued, " that the courts were designed to be an intermediate body between the people and the legislature " to keep the legislative authority within the bounds prescribed.[2] As the interpretation of the laws belongs peculiarly to the courts and the Constitution is declared to be a superior law which must be regarded by the courts as paramount, it follows that any law contrary to the provision of this instrument must be set aside as invalid. This does not mean, Hamilton thought, a superiority of the judicial over the legislative power; it only means that the will of the people shall prevail and that the courts are the better interpreters of that will. " Where the will of the legislature, declared in its statutes, stands in opposition to that of the people, declared in the Constitution, the judges ought to be governed by the latter rather than the former. They ought to regulate their decisions by the fundamental laws, rather than by those which are not fundamental." [8] Hamilton admitted that to a certain degree this was a rule of construction not derived

[1] *The Federalist,* p. 521.　　　　　　　[2] *Ibid.,* p. 521.

[8] *Ibid.,* p. 522.

from any positive law.   Though neither constitutional provision nor legislative enactment granted such power to the
courts, the theory of a Constitution with limitations, however, required that the courts follow this practice in the interpretation of the laws.   The theory of judicial nullification had found a masterful champion.   The decision of
the Supreme Court in the case of Marbury *vs.* Madison was
not only foreshadowed in this number of the Federalist, but
the principle of the case was so fully thought out that the
way for Marshall in the actual application of the principle
was comparatively easy.

Hamilton found the charge against the federal judiciary
under the plan of the Constitution to be that

The authority of the proposed Supreme Court of the United
States, which is to be a separate and independent body, will be
superior to that of the legislature.   The power of construing
the laws according to the spirit of the Constitution, will enable
that court to mould them into whatever shape it may think
proper; especially as its decision will not be in any manner
subject to the revision or correction of the legislative body.
This is as unprecedented as it is dangerous.   In Britain the
judicial power, in the last resort, resides in the House of Lords,
which is a branch of the legislature; and this part of the British
government has been imitated in the state constitutions in
general.   The Parliament of Great Britain, and the legislatures of the several states, can at any time rectify, by law, the
exceptional decisions of their respective courts.   But the errors
and usurpations of the Supreme Court of the United States
will be uncontrollable and remediless.[1]

These charges Hamilton disposed of as " made up altogether
of false reasoning upon misconceived facts." [2]

---

[1] *The Federalist*, p. 539.   [2] *Ibid.*, p. 540.

Several other men, in the debates preceding the adoption of the Constitution, expressed views in favor of the exercise of this power by the courts. Marshall in Virginia stated that " if they (the legislature) were to make a law not warranted by any of the powers enumerated, it would be considered by the judges as an infringement of the Constitution which they are to guard. They would not consider such a law as coming under their jurisdiction. They would declare it void." [1] Patrick Henry, one of the most formidable opponents of the Constitution, favored this principle when he said, " I take it as the highest encomium on this country, that the acts of the legislature, if unconstitutional, are liable to be opposed by the judiciary." [2] He thought this power should have been granted directly to the court. Wilson of Pennsylvania became a strong advocate of the same theory,[3] and many other opinions favoring the Hamiltonian doctrine may be found in the debates on the Constitution. These representative views are sufficient to show that there was a considerable public sentiment favorable to the nullification of legislative acts when in the judgment of the courts these acts were found to be inconsistent with the provisions of a written Constitution.

The opposition to the interference of the courts with legislative acts was weakening before a growing public sentiment in favor of this form of judicial control. And those who were inclined to be skeptical during the stormy days of 1787 and 1788 had to submit to conservative leaders, who succeeded finally in setting into motion the form of government drawn up by the Convention in Philadelphia, carrying with it at least an implied right of judicial nullification.[4]

---

[1] *Elliot's Debates,* iii, p. 553.   [2] *Ibid.,* pp. 324-325.

[3] *Ibid.* ii, p. 489.

[4] That it was probably intended to grant this right in the sections

2. The Organization of the Federal Judiciary.

Judiciary Act of 1789. An act organizing the courts of the United States was passed by both houses of Congress and approved by President Washington on the 24th of September, 1789.[1] The Supreme Court was to consist of a Chief Justice and five associate justices, and inferior courts were instituted in districts comprising certain designated groups of states.[2] The jurisdiction of the federal courts and the realm of judicial duties were more definitely outlined than was possible in the draft of the Constitution. The twenty-fifth section of this act is remarkable. The national legislature herein explicitly recognized the right of a state court to declare laws of the United States void, subject to an appeal to the Supreme Court of the United States wherein it was intended to vest revisory powers over all decisions affecting the validity of laws or treaties of the federal government.[3]

of the Constitution defining judicial authority is indicated in a letter of Gouverneur Morris to Timothy Pickering relative to the draft of the Constitution which Morris prepared and submitted for final approval. Morris was known to incline toward the doctrines of Hamilton and directly favor the policy of protecting the rights of property against the spirit of democracy. On the intent of the language used in the Constitution regarding the federal judiciary Morris writes, " having rejected redundant and equivocal terms, I believed it to be as clear as our language would permit; excepting, nevertheless, a part of what relates to the judiciary. On that subject, conflicting opinions had been maintained with so much professional astuteness, that it became necessary to select phrases, which expressing my own notions would not alarm others, nor shock their self-love, and to the best of my recollection, this was the only part which passed without cavil." Sparks, *Life of Morris*, iii, p. 323; also i, p. 284.

[1] *United States Statutes at Large*, i, pp. 73-93.

[2] *Ibid.*, sections 1 and 2.

[3] It was enacted " that a final judgment or decree in any suit, in the highest court of law or equity of a state in which a decision in the

An inauspicious beginning. The appointments made by President Washington to fill the positions designated by the Judiciary Act included several very able lawyers and jurists.[1] John Jay was eminently fitted for Chief Justice. Wilson, Cushing, Harrison, Blair and Rutledge were five strong associates. In a letter to Madison the President spoke of his " solicitude for drawing the first characters of the union into the judiciary." [2] He considered the judicial department essential to the stability of the political system of the country and thought it was his duty to nominate such men as would give dignity and prestige to the national government.[3]

Notwithstanding the wide constitutional authority enjoyed and a group of strong judges, the Supreme Court was slow in attaining a position of prominence in the na-

suit could be had, where is drawn in question the validity of a treaty or statute of, or an authority exercised under the United States and the decision is against their validity; or where is drawn in question the validity of a statute or an authority exercised under any state, on the ground of their being repugnant to the Constitution, treaties, or the laws of the United States and the decision is in favor of their validity, or where is drawn in question the construction of any clause of the Constitution, or of a treaty, or a statute of, or commission held under the United States, and the decision is against the title, right, privilege or exemption specially set up or claimed by either party, under such clause of the said Constitution, treaty, statute or commission, may be re-examined and reversed or affirmed in the Supreme Court of the United States upon a writ of error." *Ibid.*, pp. 85, 86.

[1] William Cushing, Chief Justice for the state of Massachusetts; James Wilson, foremost among lawyers and jurists of Pennsylvania; Robert H. Harrison, Chief Justice for the state of Maryland; John Blair, a Virginia judge; John Rutledge, a South Carolina patriot. Harrison having declined, James Iredell, one of the leading lawyers of North Carolina, was appointed in his stead.

[2] Sparks, *Life and Writings of Washington*, x, p. 26.

[3] *Ibid.*, pp. 34, 35.

tional government.   Chief Justice Jay resigned after only
a few years' service, and when tendered a reappointment by
President Adams in 1800, wrote: " I left the bench perfectly convinced that under a system so defective it would
not obtain the energy, weight, and dignity which was essential to its affording due support to the national government; nor acquire the public confidence and respect which,
as the last resort of the justice of the nation, it should
possess.   Hence I am induced to doubt both the propriety
and the expediency of my returning to the bench under the
present system." [1]   On August 5th, 1792, Edmund Randolph, the Attorney General, wrote to Washington

It is much to be regretted, that the judiciary, in spite of their
apparent firmness in annulling the pension law, are not what
sometime hence they will be, a resource against the infractions
of the Constitution on the one hand, and a steady asserter of
federal rights on the other.   So crude is our judiciary system,
so jealous are our state judges of their authority, so ambiguous
is the language of the Constitution, that the most probable
quarter, from which an alarming discontent may proceed, is
the rivalship of these two orders of judges.[2]

The reaction which was felt immediately after the adoption of the Constitution was taking a firm hold upon the
people, with the result that the powers of the state courts
were growing at the expense of federal authority.   From
1790 to 1800 only six cases were decided by the court involving questions of constitutional law,[3] and Marshall on

---

[1] Letter to President Adams, January 2, 1801, Pellew, *Life of Jay*,
pp. 337, 338.

[2] Sparks, *Life and Writings of Washington*, x, p. 513.

[3] Hayburn's Case, 2 Dallas, 410, 1792, *cf. infra*, p. 47; Chisholm's
Executor *vs.* Georgia, 2 Dallas, 419, 1793, *cf. infra*, p. 48; Hylton *vs.*

his appointment to the Supreme Bench in 1801 found but a few cases awaiting adjudication. The Supreme Court had an inauspicious beginning, and there were very few indications of those remarkable powers which this tribunal began to exercise under the masterly direction of Chief Justice Marshall.

Opinion of Madison. That the Supreme Court was expected to have authority to interpret the laws of Congress and of the states, as well as the federal Constitution, was never open to question. But that this court was to have the sole authority to place a final interpretation upon the Constitution, in such a manner that its mandate was above that of Congress, does not appear to be confirmed in the arguments over the question whether the power of removal ought to be placed in the hands of the President. Madison thought that a decision with regard to a doubtful part of the Constitution, " may come with as much propriety from the legislature as any other department of government." [1]   It was his belief that such a decision would become the permanent exposition of the Constitution.[2]   When the opposition was raised that the legislature had no right to expound the .Constitution, but must defer all doubtful questions of constitutional interpretation to the judiciary, Madison replied, " I beg to know upon what principle it can be contended that any one department draws from the Constitution greater powers than another, in marking out the limits of the powers of the several departments." [3]   In fact,

United States, 3 Dallas, 171, 1796, a federal tax on carriages held to be no direct tax; Hollingsworth *vs.* Virginia, 3 Dallas, 378, 1798, the procedure in the adoption of the eleventh amendment upheld as constitutional; Calder *vs.* Bull, 3 Dallas, 386, 1798, *cf. infra*, p. 54; Cooper *vs.* Telfair, 4 Dallas, 14, 1800, *cf. infra*, p. 55.

[1] *Elliot's Debates*, iv, p. 354, House of Representatives, June 16, 1789
[2] *Ibid.*, p. 378.   [3] *Ibid.*, p. 382.

he was unable to see how the question at issue could come before the judges. In reply to the contention that an act of Congress might be ignored by the courts, Madison emphatically declared that " nothing has yet been offered to invalidate the doctrine that the meaning of the Constitution may as well be ascertained by the legislature as by the judicial authority." [1] No one appeared to deny that Congress might interpret the Constitution, and give a construction of its own which the judiciary would be in duty bound to respect and sanction. The power was not yet recognized in the high court of justice to disregard a direct mandate from Congress.

Hayburn's Case. The first case touching the relation of the departments of the government of the United States to come before the federal courts was Hayburn's case. [2] An attempt was made by an act of Congress to authorize judges of the circuit court to receive and determine upon certain claims of widows and orphans and to regulate the claims to invalid pensions. [3] In the circuit court for the district of New York, Justices Jay, Cushing and Duane gave the opinion, " that neither the legislature nor the executive branch can constitutionally assign to the judicial any duties, but such as are properly judicial, and to be performed in a judicial manner." [4] In deference to the intention of the legislature the judges agreed to execute the act in the capacity of commissioners. In the circuit court

---

[1] *Elliot's Debates,* iv, p. 399.

[2] 2 Dallas, p. 409, 1792. Certain portions of my article on " The Political Theories of the Supreme Court from 1789-1835 " published in the *Political Science Review,* February, 1908, are used in the following pages, by special permission.

[3] *United States Statutes at Large,* i, pp. 243-245, March 23, 1792.

[4] 2 Dallas, 410.

for the district of Pennsylvania, Justices Wilson, Blair and Peters held that the whole legislative power is not vested in Congress. The Constitution as the " supreme law of the land " which all judicial officers of the United States are bound, by oath or affirmation, to support, vests judicial power in the courts.[1] The judges were unanimously of the opinion that the act of Congress placed duties upon the judiciary which were not of a judicial nature and were not vested by the Constitution in the courts, and that a revision and control of acts of the judges by either executive or legislature as provided by the act was radically inconsistent with the independence of judicial power.[2] In the circuit court for the district of North Carolina, Justices Iredell and Sitgreaves held that since the decision of the court is not final, but may be at least suspended in its operation by the Secretary of War, the judicial authority is subjected to a revision which must be considered to be unwarranted by the Constitution. And the Justices claimed, " that no decision of any court of the United States can under any circumstance, in our opinion, agreeable to the Constitution, be liable to a reversion, or even suspension, by the legislature, itself, in whom no judicial power of any kind appears to be vested, but the important one relative to impeachments." [3]

During the time that the case was under consideration, Congress passed another act [4] making a decision of the court unnecessary, but the notes of the justices indicated the position which was soon to be firmly upheld in later decisions more directly to the point.

In Conflict with Georgia.   In 1793, the court became in-

---

[1] 2 Dallas, 411.   [2] *Ibid.*, 411, 412.   [3] *Ibid.*, 413.
[4] *United States Statutes at Large*, i, pp. 324, 325, Feb. 28, 1793.

volved in a bitter controversy with the state of Georgia, with the result that the main contention of one of its decisions was directly overthrown by an amendment to the Constitution. Hamilton, Marshall and Madison had expressed the opinion that the highest authority of a state could not be called before the bar of a federal court.[1] Nevertheless Georgia was sued and on appeal to the Supreme Court, Edmund Randolph, the Attorney General, argued that unless the state of Georgia caused an appearance to be entered, in behalf of the state, judgment should be directed against the state and damages awarded.[2] Although the Attorney General accepted the doctrine of state sovereignty, he did not regard a submission to the authority of the Supreme Court as a degradation of sovereignty. On refusal to accept service, judgment was entered against the state in a decision which vigorously maintained the principle of national sovereignty. Justice Blair claimed in his opinion that " when a state, by adopting the Constitution has agreed to be amenable to the judicial power of the United States, she has, in that respect, given up her right of sovereignty." [3] Justice Wilson thought the question might be resolved to the maxim " Do the people of the United States form a nation?" and asserted positively that in the adoption of the Constitution the individual states had renounced any claim that they might have had on the possession of sovereign powers. He maintained that sovereignty in a strict sense belonged to the people of the United States,

[1] For opinion of Hamilton, see *The Federalist*, no. lxxxi, pp. 545, 546; opinion of Marshall, 3 *Elliot's Debates*, 555, " I hope that no gentleman will think that a state will be called at the bar of a federal court "; opinion of Madison, *Ibid.*, 522.

[2] Chisholm's Executor *vs.* the State of Georgia. 2 Dallas, 419.

[3] 2 Dallas, 452.

and that neither the states nor the federal authorities could lawfully claim this high prerogative. It was his opinion that Georgia was not a sovereign state, and since she had granted a full measure of general powers to the central government, she therefore made herself amenable to the judicial authority under the Constitution.[1] This direct and forceful statement of the nationalist doctrine was so much in contradiction to the views held in the states that they added an amendment to the Constitution which was expected to put beyond reach of the Supreme Court most of the important controversies between the states.[2] In a notable dissenting opinion, Justice Iredell denied the soundness of the arguments of the majority of the court and held that no such action against a state could be legally maintained.[3]

The attitude of the court in assuming jurisdiction in the case was regarded as unconstitutional and extra-judicial. It was feared that a precedent might be set, which " would effectually destroy the retained sovereignty of the states, and would actually tend in its operation to annihilate the very shadow of state government and to render them but tributary corporations to the government of the United States." [4] The court rendered its opinion on February

[1] 2 Dallas, 453 *et seq.*

[2] " The judicial power of the United States shall not be construed to extend to any suit in law or equity, commenced or prosecuted against one of the United States by citizens of another state, or by citizens or subjects of any foreign state."—XI Amendment.

[3] 2 Dallas, 429 *et seq.*

[4] Ames, *State Documents on Federal Relations*, p. 7. The collection of documents by Professor Ames is one of the first works to make accessible to students of American History the official action of the states relative to certain judicial controversies. The historical introductions to the conflicts with the federal judiciary and the bibliographies for each controversy are especially valuable.

18th, 1793. The whole country was aroused; the worst fears of those who had opposed the adoption of the Constitution were to be realized. The eleventh amendment was immediately proposed and hurriedly carried through Congress. The decision of the court was almost unanimously regarded as " dangerous to the peace, safety and independence of the states." [1]   A bill which passed the Georgia house of assembly, but apparently was not favorably acted on by the senate, declared that federal marshals attempting to execute the writ of the Supreme Court against the state of Georgia " are hereby declared to be guilty of felony, and shall suffer death without the benefit of clergy by being hanged." [2]   A serious conflict was thus avoided by the proposal and adoption of the eleventh amendment.

Conflict with New Hampshire.   Again, as early as 1793, the federal judiciary came into a conflict with one of the New England states. The case grew out of the capture of a vessel, the Susanna, by the brigantine McClary. The cargo of the vessel was condemned and ordered to be sold by the admiralty court of New Hampshire. [3]   In a trial before the federal Court of Appeals in cases of capture, a decision was rendered October 1777, adverse to the contention of the state. The case was dropped until 1793, when an issue was brought before the circuit court of the United States for the district of New Hampshire, and the decision of the Court of Appeals was upheld. On appeal to the Supreme Court of the United States the decision of the inferior court was affirmed. The legislature of the state, immediately after the decision of the circuit court, issued a

---

[1] Resolves of Massachusetts, *Massachusetts Archives* (MS.), ix, 103.

[2] Ames, *op. cit.*, p. 10.

[3] For history of this case see Penhallow *vs.* Doane's Administrators, 3 Dallas, 54-79.

remonstrance practically asserting the sovereignty of the state and denying the jurisdiction of the federal courts.[1] Following the decision of the Supreme Court, the legislature on February 27th, 1795, sent another communication to Congress objecting seriously to " a violation of state independence and an unwarrantable encroachment in the courts of the United States." [2] The remonstrance contained a complete denial of a federal judicial authority superior to that of the state, prior to 1788. The legislature regarded Congress as merely an advisory body, and it resolved " not to submit the laws made before the existence of the present government by this (then independent state) to the adjudication of any power on earth." [3] The legislature also threatened to resist an attempt to execute an " unconstitutional decree of a court instituted by a former Congress, and which, in its effects, would unsettle property and tear up the laws of the several states." [4]

Submitting the report of the committee to which these remonstrances were referred, Madison noted, " that the subject of said memorial being of a nature wholly judicial. and having undergone a course of judicial investigation and of final decision by the Supreme Court of the United States, the committee have conceived themselves precluded from all inquiry into the particular merits of the case; nor can perceive any ground on which legislative interference could be proper." [5]

The opposition, as in the Georgia case. came to be identified with the radical states-rights' party. And as this party grew to be more out of harmony with the trend of public sentiment in the rapidly growing country, the opposition

[1] *American State Papers*, Miscellaneous, vol. i, p. 79.

[2] *Ibid.*, p. 124.   [3] *Ibid.*, p. 124.

[4] *Ibid.*, p. 124.   [5] *Ibid.*, p. 123.

to the practice of judicial nullification lost that respectability which, under normal conditions, might have tended to hold the courts in check in the exercise of the power to declare legislative acts unconstitutional.

In 1795, Justice Patterson in the circuit court of the United States for the Pennsylvania district discussed the relative position of the legislature, the courts and the Constitution.[1] The Justice assumed a very emphatic tone.

What is a Constitution? It is the form of government, delineated by the mighty hand of the people, in which certain fixed principles of fundamental laws are established. The Constitution is certain and fixed; it contains the permanent will of the people, and is the supreme law of the land; it is paramount to the power of the legislature and can be revoked or altered only by the authority that made it. The lifegiving principle and the death-doing stroke must proceed from the same hand. What are the legislatures? Creatures of the Constitution; they owe their existence to the Constitution; they derive their powers from the Constitution; it is their commission; and, therefore, all their acts must be conformable to it, or else they will be void. The Constitution is the work or will of the people, themselves, in their original, sovereign, and unlimited capacity. Law is the work or will of the legislature in their derivative and subordinate capacity. The one is the work of the creator and the other of the creature. The Constitution fixes limits to the exercise of legislative authority, and prescribes the orbit within which it must move. In short, gentlemen, the Constitution is the sun of the political system, around which all legislative, executive and judicial bodies must revolve. Whatever may be the case in other countries, yet in this there can be no doubt that every act of the legislature, repugnant to the Constitution is absolutely void.[2]

[1] Vanhorne's Lessee *vs*. Dorrance, 2 Dallas, 304.
[2] 2 Dallas, 308.

An opinion on an ex post facto law. In 1798, a case was appealed to the Supreme Court to test the validity of a retroactive law passed by the legislature of Connecticut.[1] Justice Chase was satisfied that the Supreme Court had no jurisdiction to determine whether any law of the state legislature contrary to the state constitution was void, but declined to express an opinion whether they could declare void an act of Congress contrary to the federal Constitution.[2] Justice Iredell, whose views in the North Carolina case of Den *vs.* Singleton have been noted, dealt with this issue in a concurring opinion. It has been the policy of all the American states, he observed, to define the objects of the legislative power and to fix the boundaries for the exercise of this power. " If any act of Congress, or of the legislature of a state, violates those constitutional provisions, it is unquestionably void; though I admit, that as the authority to declare it void is of a delicate and awful nature, the court will never resort to that authority but in a clear and urgent case." [3] After denying that courts may set aside laws because of an inconsistency with the principle of natural justice, Iredell summarized his views in two propositions:

First, if the legislature pursue the authority delegated to them their acts are valid. Secondly, if they transgress the boundaries of that authority, their acts are invalid. In the former case they exercise the discretion vested in them by the people, to whom alone they are responsible for the faithful discharge of their trust; but in the latter case, they violate a fundamental law, which must be our guide whenever we are called upon as judges to determine the validity of a legislative act.[4]

---

[1] Calder *vs.* Bull. 3 Dallas, 386.   [2] *Ibid.,* 387, 388.

[3] *Ibid.,* 399.   [4] *Ibid.,* 399.

The issue was again raised on an appeal from the circuit court of the United States for the district of Georgia.[1] Under acts of the Georgia legislature one Cooper and several others had been expelled from the state, and their property had been confiscated. It was argued on trial that the acts of the state were repugnant to the constitution of Georgia and therefore void. The circuit court refused to set aside the state laws in question and the Supreme Court affirmed this decision. Justice Chase observed,

Although it is alleged that all acts of the legislature, in direct opposition to the prohibitions of the Constitution, would be void; yet, it still remains a question, where the power resides to declare it void? It is, indeed, a general opinion, it is expressly admitted by all this bar, and some of the judges have individually in the circuits, decided, that the Supreme Court can declare an act of Congress to be unconstitutional and therefore invalid; but there is no adjudication of the Supreme Court itself upon the point. I concur, however, in the general sentiment with reference to the period, when the existing Constitution came into operation.[2]

The timid and doubtful attitude concerning this power was very evident in the first cases which came before the court. " To be obliged to act," said one Justice, " contrary either to the obvious direction of Congress, or to a constitutional principle, in our judgment equally obvious excited feelings in us which we hope never to experience again." [3]   The way the court was likely to decide when the direct issue presented itself was indicated in the decisions

---

[1] Cooper *vs.* Telfair, 4 Dallas, 14, 1800.
[2] *Ibid.,* 19.
[3] Hayburn's Case, 2 Dallas, 412.

of the state courts, in the arguments in favor of the adoption of the Constitution, and in a few federal decisions.

The members of the Supreme Court were finally led to favor a power of review of all federal and state laws, and to insist upon declaring the same void when deemed to be contrary to the provisions of the federal Constitution. It was left for Chief Justice Marshall, whose judicial opinions were always expressed in the most definite and lucid style, to clarify and develop the arguments in favor of this feature of the American system. But before the Supreme Court was called upon to deal directly with the issue, a very important controversy arose which brought out clearly the prevailing sentiment of the time regarding judicial authority.

3. The Kentucky and Virginia Resolutions.

In the discussion which arose over the Alien and Sedition laws, so bitterly opposed by the anti-federalists, the resolutions drawn up by Thomas Jefferson, adopted by the Kentucky legislature, and submitted to the other states contained a doctrine distinctly opposed to the idea of a national sovereignty with a final interpreting organ in the central government. It was declared that the states had been united under a compact, with the reserved right of government or ultimate control in the states which became members of the compact of the Union. The resolution went on to declare " that the government created by this compact was not made the exclusive or final judge of the extent of the powers delegated to itself; since that would have made its discretion and not the Constitution, the measure of its powers; but that as in all other cases of compact among parties having no common judge, each party has an equal right to judge for itself, as well as of infractions as of the mode and measure of redress." [1] A similar resolution, somewhat less radical in spirit, was prepared by Madison and was adopted by the Virginia assembly declaring in effect " that the acts aforesaid are unconstitutional; and that the necessary and proper measures will be taken by each [state] for co-operating with this state, in maintaining unimpaired the authorities, rights, and liberties reserved to the states respectively or to the people." [2]

Replies from the States. The resolutions of these respective assemblies were branded as an " unjustifiable interference with the general government," and as " a dangerous tendency" which was to be spurned by all loyal citizens. [3] Rhode Island replied that the Constitution of the United States " vests in the federal courts, exclusively, and in the Supreme Court of the United States, ultimately, the authority of deciding on the constitutionality of any act or law of the Congress of the United States." [4] Massachusetts resolved: " that this legislature are persuaded that the decision of all cases in law and equity arising under the Constitution of the United States, and the construction of all laws made in pursuance thereof, are exclusively vested by the people in the judicial courts of the United States." The house of representatives of Pennsylvania was of the opinion that the people of the United States " have committed to the supreme judiciary of the nation the high authority of ultimately and conclusively deciding upon the constitutionality of all legislative acts."   All the other

[1] *Works of Thomas Jefferson* (Ford's edition), viii, p. 459.
[2] *Works of Madison*, iv, p. 507.
[3] Reply of Delaware to Virginia, *Elliot's Debates*, iv, p. 532.
[4] Reply of Rhode Island to Virginia, *Ibid.*, iv, p. 533.
[5] Reply of Massachusetts to Virginia, *Ibid.*, iv, p. 534.
[6] *Journal of House of Representatives of Pennsylvania*, ix, p. 198.

states that gave a reply to the resolutions thought that the duty and power as arbiter was properly and exclusively vested in the judicial department of the central government. As the legislatures of the states, so soon after the establishment of the government under the federal Constitution, came out so unanimously and unequivocally in favor of the view that the Supreme Court of the United States was vested with the full and ultimate authority to determine the validity of legislative acts of Congress, it appears useless to claim that the national court usurped authority. The states themselves had prepared the way in the precedents established before 1789. State courts had continued to exercise this right and now the highest legislative authority in each of a majority of the states sanctioned the principle of judicial nullification which the federal courts had so far hesitated to affirm.

The opponents of the wide powers claimed for the judiciary were overwhelmed by a general sentiment which upheld the courts in almost every assertion of authority, and by a complete acceptance of judicial precedents as law for future cases. All departments of government were ultimately obliged to give way to the interpretation placed upon laws by the courts, and the people generally acquiesced in the acceptance of judicial opinions as final on the constitutionality of laws. Occasional protests of injured litigants and a few criticisms of the whole theory underlying the practice are the only evidences that a few were not reconciled to this peculiar development in the realm of law and government.

Senator Breckenridge was one of those who were willing to stand out against the prevailing opinion of the time. In fact he introduced a bill to reorganize the whole judicial system of the country.[1] He opposed the doctrine that

[1] *Elliot's Debates*, iv, p. 440.

courts of justice might refuse to enforce acts of Congress and in defence of his measure he formulated a series of propositions denying the right which courts were regularly inclined to assert.   He argued,

To make the Constitution a practical system, the power of the court to annul the laws of Congress cannot possibly exist. My idea of the subject in a few words, is—that the Constitution intended a separation only of the powers vested in the three great departments, giving to each the exclusive authority of acting on the subject committed to each; that each are intended to revolve within the sphere of their own orbit, are responsible for their own motion only and are not to direct or control the course of others; that those for example, who make the laws, are presumed to have an equal attachment to and interest in the Constitution, are equally bound by oath to support it, and have an equal right to give a construction of it; that the construction of one department, of the powers particularly vested in that department, is of as high authority, at least, as the construction given it by any other department; that it is in fact more competent to that department to which such powers are exclusively confided, to decide upon the proper exercise of those powers, than any other department to which such powers are not entrusted and who are not consequently under such high and responsible obligation for their exercise; and that therefore, the legislature would have an equal right to annul the decisions of the court founded upon their construction of the Constitution.[1]

Although he found that the courts were inclined to give decisions which obstructed the operation of a law, he contended that such a law is not the less obligatory because the organ through which it was to be executed had refused its aid. On the basis of these propositions he reached the conclusion that

----

[1] *Elliot's Debates*, iv, p. 444.

a prolonged conflict between two departments of government would result in a determination of the question as to where the sovereign power of legislation resided.

4. Marshall's opinion in the case of Marbury vs. Madison.

The position of the court and the relation between the three departments of our government were determined by Chief Justice Marshall in the great case of Marbury vs. Madison.[1] Among other issues, the question arose whether the authority given to the Supreme Court by the act organizing the courts of the United States to issue writs of mandamus to public officers was warranted by the Constitution, or, in other words, whether an act, which, according to the judgment of the members of the court, was repugnant to the Constitution could become the law of the land. The court, in an opinion delivered by the Chief Justice, thought " that the question whether an act repugnant to the Constitution can become the law of the land is a question deeply interesting to the United States; but happily, not of an intricacy proportional to its interest. It seems only necessary to recognize certain principles, supposed to have been long established to decide it." [2] The people have an original right to establish the basic principles of government. Acts emanating from the people are supreme and as this authority can seldom act, the rules established by them must be regarded as permanent. " This original and supreme will organizes the government, and assigns to different departments their respective powers." [3] In the government of the United States

The powers of the legislature are defined and limited; and that those limits may not be mistaken, or forgotten, the Con-

---

[1] 1 Cranch, 137.   [2] Ibid., 175.   [3] Ibid., 176.

stitution is written. To what purpose are powers limited, and to what purpose is that limitation committed to writing, if these limits may, at any time, be passed by those intended to be restrained? . . . It is a proposition too plain to be contested, that the Constitution controls any legislative act repugnant to it; or, that the legislature may alter the Constitution by an ordinary act. Between these alternatives there is no middle ground. The Constitution is either a superior paramount law unchangeable by ordinary means, or it is on a level with ordinary acts alterable when the legislature shall please to alter it. If the former part of the alternative be true, then a legislative act contrary to the Constitution is not law; if the latter part be true, then written Constitutions are absurd attempts, on the part of the people, to limit a power in its own nature illimitable. Certainly all those who have framed written Constitutions contemplate them as forming the fundamental and paramount law of the nation, and, consequently, the theory of every such government must be, that an act of the legislature, repugnant to the Constitution, is void. This theory is essentially attached to a written constitution, and, is consequently, to be considered, by this court, as one of the fundamental principles of our society. . . . It is emphatically the province and duty of the judicial department to say what the law is. . . . If two laws conflict with each other the courts must decide on the operation of each.[1]

As between a law and the Constitution when both apply to a particular case the courts must determine which of the rules shall apply. " If then the courts are to regard the Constitution, and the Constitution is superior to any ordinary act of the legislature, the Constitution, and not such ordinary act, must govern the case to which they both apply." [2] Those who deny the principle that the Constitution

---

[1] 1 Cranch, 176, 177.   [2] *Ibid.*, 179.

is a paramount law must maintain that courts must close their eyes on the Constitution, and see only the law. Such a doctrine is held to be contrary to the nature of written Constitutions, because it would declare that an act which, according to the principles and theory of our government, is entirely void, is in practice completely obligatory. This would give a practical omnipotence to the legislature in the very face of many express restrictions. Why does a judge swear to discharge his duties agreeably to the Constitution of the United States if that Constitution forms no rule for his government? " The particular phraseology of the Constitution of the United States confirms and strengthens the principle, supposed to be essential to all written constitutions, that a law repugnant to the Constitution is void; and that the courts, as well as other departments, are bound by that instrument." [1]

This masterly opinion at once settled the doubt regarding the attitude of the court on the right of judicial nullification in a manner that was clear, definite and decisive. In it, the Chief Justice declared that the Supreme Court was the final interpreter and guardian of the federal Constitution, and formulated a theory of the separation of powers differing widely from the English system and entirely distinct from the interpretation of that system advanced by Montesquieu. [2] The decision became authority for the proposition which had already been adopted in a number of the states and which was destined to form a distinct feature of the whole political system of the United States: that a constitution is a fundamental law formulated by the people acting in their original capacity, in which the government

---

[1] 1 Cranch, 179.

[2] Montesquieu, *L'Esprit des Lois*, book xi, chapter vi.

is organized and the limits are prescribed for the exercise
of governmental power; and that the courts as interpreters
of the law are expected to preserve and defend these constitutions as inviolable acts, to be changed only by the original and supreme power—the people. Although President
Jefferson did not accept as final the opinion of the Chief
Justice, it was clearly in line with the prevailing opinion of
the time, and the reverence for law so notable among the
American people made it possible for the court to assert
and maintain its position as a final authority on the important issues of government in a long list of great cases
which came to the court for decision.

5. *The Views of Jefferson.*

The history of the rapid progress of the Supreme Court
in power and authority began with the advent of John Marshall to the Supreme Bench in 1801. This period also
marked the beginning of a determined opposition to the
court by the executive department. It is well known that
Marshall and his associates, all staunch Federalists, strengthened by the re-organization of the federal judicial system,
wrought a manifest revolution in developing the authority
and defining the duties of the central government. The re-
organization of the judicial system [1] with the sole object
of appointing to the new places justices in sympathy with
federalist doctrine, and the evident intention to foster the
development of national power through the courts, was
eminently hateful to the democratic principles of Jefferson.

The law under which the federal judicial system was re-
modeled was immediately repealed,[2] but the Supreme Court
in charge of the newly appointed Chief Justice was left un-
touched. No doubt Jefferson regarded Marshall as an able

---

[1] *United States Statutes at Large,* ii, pp. 89-100.   [2] *Ibid.,* p. 132.

jurist and felt assured that his party, by means of political pressure, and if need be by impeachment, could effectually control the courts. The bold and almost defiant decision of the court in the case of Marbury *vs.* Madison, when the judicial veto was not only unqualifiedly asserted, but the complete authority of the President over his cabinet officers was positively denied, dealt a severe blow to democratic aspirations. The power of impeachment had been held out, in the debates prior to the adoption of the Constitution, as the natural and effective method of keeping the judicial power under control. That power was now to be exercised by the majority party to prevent the interference of the courts with the undoubted will of the people. It was generally believed that " if the judges of the Supreme Court should dare as they had done, to declare an act of Congress unconstitutional, or to send a mandamus to the Secretary of the State as they had done," [1] it would be the duty of the House of Representatives and the Senate to remove them for exceeding their constitutional limits. In 1805, several Pennsylvania Justices were brought to trial, but the proceedings proved unsuccessful because the necessary two-thirds majority could not be secured. The issue was finally put to the test in the trial of Chase, who had been indiscreet and was certainly guilty of conduct unbecoming to a judicial officer. The trial was conducted unwisely, and as no criminal actions were shown in the conduct of the judge, the whole proceeding proved to be a decided failure.[2] Justice Chase was acquitted, the attitude of the court was vindicated, and the result was that Congress was not inclined to interfere in future controversies.

[1] John Quincy Adams, *Memoirs,* i, p. 322.

[2] Henry Adams, *History of the United States.* ii, chap. x, " Trial of Chase."

President Jefferson did not submit as gracefully as Congress. He ignored entirely the decision of the court in the Marbury case, referring to it later as an " obiter dissertation " of the Chief Justice.[1] He continued to follow his own interpretation of the Constitution, or that interpretation with which he thought the people were most in sympathy. He realized as probably few men of the time did, that the Supreme Court would, as a result of such decisions, become the final judge of its own authority.

His refusal to accept as final the opinion in the Marbury case and his declination to appear before the court in the Burr conspiracy trial have since been recognized as valuable precedents necessary for the independence of the executive in the American constitutional system. During the remainder of Jefferson's term, there was little provocation for conflicts between the executive and judicial departments. On his return to private life, Jefferson became an uncompromising foe of Marshall and an outspoken opponent of the practice of judicial nullification. On May 25th, 1810, writing to Madison relative to an appointment to the Supreme Court, he warned the new President against " the cunning and sophistry " of the Chief Justice, and intimated that it would be difficult to find a man with enough firmness of character to maintain his independence by the side of Marshall.[2] In a letter to Judge Tyler whose cause he was urging at this time he wrote

We have long enough suffered under the base prostitution of law to party passions in one judge, and the imbecility of another. In the hands of one the law is nothing more than an

[1] *Works of Jefferson* (Ford's edition), xii, p. 257.
[2] *Ibid.*, xi, pp. 140, 141.

ambiguous text, to be explained by his sophistry into any meaning which may subserve his personal malice. Nor can any
milk-and-water associate maintain his own dependence, and by
a firm pursuance of what the law really is, extend its protection
to the citizens or the public.[1]

He insisted that not a word in the Constitution had given
the power of final interpretation to the judges rather than
to the executive or legislative branches.

His feelings grew in intensity with every decision from
the court which affected the fundamental rights claimed by
the states. When the powerful opinions favoring national
authority, such as McCulloch *vs.* Maryland, Darthmouth
College *vs.* Woodward and Cohens *vs.* Virginia, followed in
close succession, his letters, containing frequent references
to the courts, became bitter and vindictive. To Judge
Spencer Roane who granted a modified form of the federal
judicial veto he wrote, September 6, 1819, that

In denying the right they usurp of exclusively explaining the
Constitution, I go further than you do. . . . If this opinion
be sound, then indeed is our Constitution a complete *felo de se.*
For intending to establish three departments, co-ordinate and
independent, that they might check and balance one another,
it has given, according to this opinion, to one of them alone,
the right to prescribe rules for the government of the others,
and to that one too, which is unelected by, and independent of
the nation. For experience has already shown that the impeachment it has provided is not even a scarecrow.[2]

The Constitution on this hypothesis, is a mere thing of wax
in the hands of the judiciary, which they may twist and

[1] *Works of Jefferson,* xi, p. 142.
[2] *Ibid.,* xii, pp. 136, 137.

shape into any form they please.[1] According to Jefferson's construction of the Constitution, each department was meant to be truly independent and to have an equal right to decide for itself what was the meaning of the Constitution in the cases submitted to its action.

In 1820 a work was submitted to Jefferson in which the judges were considered as the ultimate arbiters of all constitutional questions. This, Jefferson held, was a " very dangerous doctrine indeed, and one which would place us under the despotism of an oligarchy. Our judges are as honest as other men, and not more so. They have with others, the same passions for party, for power, and the privilege of their corps." [2] Their power, he thought, is the more dangerous because they are in office for life, and not responsible, as the legislative and executive departments are, to the people through the elective control. It is respectfully submitted that the Constitution restrains the authority of the judges to judicial duties as it does the executive and legislative to their respective duties. But regardless of this principle, the judges have undertaken to dictate to the executive in the discharge of his duties.

Jefferson regularly expressed the fear that the courts of the United States were attempting to break down the constitutional barriers between the co-ordinate powers of the state and the Union. In his autobiography prepared in 1821, Jefferson discussed the draft of the constitution submitted to the Philadelphia Convention and certain amendments thereto. He then referred to an amendment which was overlooked at the time, and, in the omission of which lurked the danger that was leading to the destruction of the combination of national powers in a general government and independent powers in the states.[3] This amendment

---

[1] *Works of Jefferson*, xii, pp. 137, 138.   [2] *Ibid.*, p. 163.

[3] *Works*, pp. 120, 121.

which was intended to submit the federal judiciary to a practical and impartial control, Jefferson regarded as indispensable to the continuance of federal government in the United States.[1] He wrote

It is not enough that honest men are appointed judges. All know the influence of interest on the mind of man, and how unconsciously his judgment is warped by influence. To this bias add that of the *esprit de corps,* of their peculiar maxim and creed that " it is the office of a good judge to enlarge his jurisdiction," and the absence of responsibility, and how can we expect impartial decisions between the general government, of which they are themselves so eminent a part and an individual state from which they have nothing to hope or fear. We have seen too, that, contrary to all correct example, they are in the habit of going out of the question before them, to throw an anchor ahead and grapple further hold for future advances of power. They are then in fact the corps of sappers and miners, steadily working to undermine the independent rights of the states, and to consolidate all power in the hands of that government in which they have so important free-hold estate.[2]

He became more and more convinced as decision after decision was announced defining the powers and duties of the various departments of government in the calm and commanding logic of Marshall, that the judges would soon be in a position " to lay all things at their feet."

[1] *Works,* pp. 121, 122.   [2] *Ibid.,* p. 122.

CHAPTER III

EXTENSION OF FEDERAL JUDICIAL AUTHORITY

1. *Restrictions upon the political power of the judiciary*

AT the opening of the nineteenth century, the Supreme Court, guided by a Constitution which rather vaguely defined its duties, had become the final interpreter of its own authority as well as the authority of the other departments. To have abused this prerogative, especially at the beginning, would have meant a speedy decline in the high authority of the court. Soon after its organization, the court experienced a bitter reversal which pressed home the realization that its powers must be worked out with great caution. Important questions of governmental policy were sure to be brought before this tribunal for solution. To guard the position of the federal judiciary, and to keep it out of politics as far as the exigencies of the case would allow, there was recognized in the distribution of powers by the Constitution a realm which the court ought not to enter. Chief Justice Marshall in the case of Marbury *vs*. Madison said, "by the Constitution of the United States, the President is invested with certain important political powers, in the exercise of which he is to use his own discretion, and is accountable only to his country in his political character and to his own conscience."[1] It was also held that "where the heads of departments are the political or confidential agents of the executive, merely to execute the will of the

[1] 1 Cranch, 165.

President, or rather to act in cases in which the executive possesses a constitutional or legal discretion, nothing can be more perfectly clear than that their acts are only politically examinable." [1]   Again, in the case of Foster *vs.* Neilson, Marshall held that

In a controversy between two nations concerning a national boundary, it is scarcely possible that the courts of either should refuse to abide by the measures adopted by its own government. . . . The judiciary is not that department of government to which the assertion of its interests against foreign powers is confided; and its duty commonly is to decide upon individual rights, according to those principles which the political departments of the nation have established. . . . We think, then, however individual judges might construe the treaty of St. Ildefonso, it is the province of the court to conform its decisions to the will of the legislature if that will has been clearly expressed. [2]

The courts here accepted as final an act of Congress determining a boundary dispute with Spain concerning the territory of Florida, regardless of the fact that, according to the Constitution, the President and Senate were intrusted with the control of foreign relations.   The so-called realm of political issues or political powers has served as a refuge on a few occasions when a definite determination would have involved the court directly in political controversy.

Justice Chase recognized a further limitation upon the right of the federal courts to nullify legislative acts.   " The legislative power of every nation," said he, " can only be restrained by its own constitution; and it is the duty of the courts of justice not to question the validity of any law

[1] 1 Cranch, 166.   [2] 2 Peters, 306, 307.

made in pursuance of the constitution." [1] The justice of a legislative act could not therefore be questioned by the courts unless there was an infringement of constitutional authority. The idea of rejecting laws contrary to natural justice or as infractions of the law of nature, though repeated a number of times by members of the Supreme Court, did not come to be regarded as 'sufficient ground to declare legislative acts void. [2]

From the nature of its position and the principles underlying its organization, the Supreme Court refused to consider any constitutional question unless a case was presented by an individual demanding redress. Several of the States, notably Massachusetts and New Hampshire, required the judges of the higher courts to give opinions upon the constitutionality of measures in advance to the executive or the legislature. [3] But this idea was generally regarded as contrary to the principle of judicial independence and the separation of powers and was therefore rejected. Various attempts were made to secure the opinion of the courts on the constitutionality of proposed measures. Soon after the establishment of the national government,

[1] Ware *vs.* Hylton, 3 Dallas, 223.

[2] In the case of Calder *vs.* Bull, two years later, Justice Chase himself rendered the opinion that "there are certain vital principles in our free republican government, which will determine and overrule an apparent and flagrant abuse of legislative power. . . . An act of the legislature (for I cannot call it a law) contrary to the first great principles of the social compact, cannot be considered a rightful exercise of legislative authority." 3 Dallas, 388.

[3] The constitution of Massachusetts, 1780, provided that "each branch of the legislature, as well as the governor and council, shall have authority to require the opinions of the Justices of the supreme judicial court upon important questions of law, and upon solemn occasions." Poore, Charters and Constitutions, pt. i, chap. iii, art. ii, pp. 968, 969; the constitution of New Hampshire, 1784, included a similar section. *Ibid.,* pt. ii, p. 1290.

Washington asked the opinion of the judges of the Supreme Court upon various questions arising out of the treaty with France.[1] The judges hesitated to express their opinions on the points referred to them and deemed it improper to enter the field of politics by giving opinions on questions not growing out of the regular case.[2]

2. The determination of the relation between nation and state

The most fundamental and by far the most difficult question that came before the court for determination was the legal relation between the governments of the states and the government of the United States. To the court, as the final interpreter of the Constitution, most of the important controversies affecting this relation were appealed. The extra-legal methods followed throughout the Revolution, in the establishment of the Confederation and especially in the course of the formation and adoption of the Constitution led to almost insuperable difficulties, which the court from the nature of its position was obliged to settle. The political nature of the issue did not seem to affect the court's consideration. Ware *vs.* Hylton[3] was the first case in which this relation was directly discussed. The difficulty arose over the conflict between a law of the state of Virginia confiscating the property of British subjects and a section of the treaty of 1783 which provided for the payment of debts due British creditors. Justice Chase delivered the opinion of the court, and upheld the section of the treaty of 1783, regardless of the law of Virginia. He held that a treaty, according to the Constitution of the United States, is the

[1] United States *vs.* Ferreira, 13 Howard, 40; Sparks, *Works of Washington*, x, p. 359.

[2] Marshall, *Life of Washington*, v, p. 441.   [3] 3 Dallas, 199.

supreme law of the land.   Nevertheless, in this opinion the
Justice announced a doctrine which later became the pronounced theory of the states-rights adherents.   The Justice said:

In June, 1776, the convention of Virginia formally declared
that Virginia was a free, sovereign and independent state;
and on the fourth of July, 1776, following, the United States,
in Congress assembled, declared the thirteen United Colonies
free and independent states. . . . I consider this as a
declaration not that the United Colonies jointly, in a collective
capacity, were independent states, but that each of them had
a right to govern itself by its own authority, and its own laws,
without any control from any other power on earth. . . .
I have ever considered it as an established doctrine of the
United States . . . that all laws made by the legislatures
of the several states after the Declaration of Independence,
were the laws of sovereign and independent governments.[1]

This was a definite recognition of state sovereignty during
the period following the declaration of independence, and
only a little advance was necessary to lead to the Kentucky
resolutions, the Hartford Convention and direct nullification by South Carolina.   This theory, even in a more pronounced form, was continuously presented in the arguments
of cases, but it received little encouragement in the decisions
given by the court.   Even Justice Chase determined that
the treaty of 1783, declared to be the supreme law of the
land by the Constitution, must be upheld, and the law of
Virginia, repugnant thereto, declared null and void.   Hereafter the doctrines of the federalists dominated the court to
such a degree that practically all of the great cases were
determined in favor of the national government, upholding

[1] 3 Dallas, 224, 225

almost exclusively the powers of the central authorities.[1] Curiously enough most of these opinions were delivered and some striking advances toward the enlargement of federal authority were made under democratic administrations, when the theory of a strict interpretation of the provisions of the Constitution was one of the principles of the party in power.

3. *Limitations on the powers of the states*

The Supreme Court not only asserted the right to determine the validity of laws of Congress and to set aside state laws in conflict with express provisions of the federal Constitution, treaties or laws, but under the direction of Marshall this tribunal was also inclined to place other decided limitations upon the realm of state authority. The Constitution contains a provision that the states shall not impair the obligation of contracts.[2]   On the basis of this provision the court held, in the case of Fletcher *vs.* Peck,[3] that when a law is in its nature a contract, a repeal of the law cannot divest rights acquired under the law.   It was the unanimous opinion of the court that " the state of Georgia was restrained either by general principles which are common to our free institutions, or by the particular provisions of the Constitution of the United States, from passing a law whereby " an estate could be constitutionally and legally impaired.[4]   An attitude of extreme caution was shown in

---

[1] It was in this case that John Marshall appeared as counsel and in his argument expressed the opinion that " the legislative authority of any country, can only be restrained by its own municipal constitution: this is a principle that springs from the very nature of society and the judicial authority can have no right to question the validity of a law, unless such a jurisdiction is expressly given by the Constitution."   3 Dallas, 211.

[2] Art. i, sec. x.   [3] 6 Cranch, 87.   [4] *Ibid.,* 139.

the opinion delivered in this case, and a principle was stated
by which courts were to be guided in dealing with the constitutionality of legislative acts.   The Chief Justice held
that

The question whether a law be void for its repugnancy to the
Constitution, is at all times a question of much delicacy,
which ought seldom, if ever, to be decided in the affirmative
in a doubtful case.   .   .   .   It is not on slight implication and
vague conjecture that the legislature is to be pronounced to
have transcended its powers, and its acts to be considered
void.   The opposition between the Constitution and the law
should be such that the judge feels a clear and strong conviction of their incompatibility with each other.[1]

The case of Dartmouth College *vs.* Woodward[2] extended
the limitation already imposed.   It was therein held that a
charter granted to a private institution or corporation was
a contract, and that such contract could not be impaired by
future legislation unless the right had been reserved in the
original grant.   By a series of acts the legislature of New
Hampshire had reorganized the form of control and man-
agement of Dartmouth College, which had been conducted
thus far under the provisions of a charter granted by the
King of England.   The state claimed that there was no
limitation in the constitution of the state nor the fundamental law of the United States to interfere with the control of such corporations.   On the basis of that clause in
the Constitution which denied the right of states to impair
the obligation of contracts, the case was appealed to the
Supreme Court of the United States.   The Attorney-
General in behalf of the state claimed that this provision
was intended to affect private contracts only, and the rights

[1] 6 Cranch, 128.   [2] 4 Wheaton, 518.

acquired under them. He regarded the appeal as an attempt to extend the obvious meaning of the Constitution and to apply it by a species of legal fiction to a class of cases which had always been under government control.[1] Chief Justice Marshall, following the reasoning of Webster, the counsel for the old corporation, gave it as his opinion that the state had attempted to divest the property of a private corporation, and that this particular type of legislation was meant to be prohibited by the federal Constitution. These two cases formed the beginning of a most extensive series of restrictions upon state legislation, on account of the fact that a great majority of laws may be attacked on the ground of an infringement of property rights—a good part of which was now placed entirely beyond the control of the state legislature.

The clause in the Constitution which authorizes Congress to regulate commerce was likewise so interpreted as to take a large part of commercial relations out of the jurisdiction of the state. The court defined commerce to include traffic and general commercial intercourse, and held that the primary regulation of such intercourse belongs to Congress and not to the states. As a result of the decision in Gibbons vs. Ogden,[2] the acts of the legislature of the state of New York, granting to Livingston and Fulton the exclusive navigation of all waters by fire or steam within the jurisdiction of the state were held to be repugnant to the Constitution, and the control of all such navigable waters placed within the jurisdiction of the federal government. In the case of Brown vs. Maryland,[3] the court maintained that a tax on the original importer of an article before it had become a part of the general property of the state was a tax

[1] 4 Wheaton, 609.   [2] 9 Wheaton, 1.   [3] 12 Wheaton, 419.

on commerce and therefore prohibited by the Constitution. The states had already been prohibited from taxing the bank of the United States,[1] on the ground that the power to tax involved the power to destroy; that the power to destroy might defeat and render useless the power to create. and that there was a plain repugnance in conferring on one government a power to control the constitutional measures of the other. " Whenever the terms in which a power is granted to Congress, or the nature of the power, require that it should be exercised exclusively by Congress, the subject is as completely taken from the state legislatures as if they had been expressly forbidden to act on it." [2]   On the great subjects of contracts, commerce, and taxation, the state governments were forced to submit to very important restrictions imposed by the Constitution as interpreted by the federal Supreme Court.

4. The development of the doctrine of implied powers

At the same time that the Supreme Court was establishing its position as the final court of appeal in all cases of conflict of authorities, it was strengthening the position of the national government by the development of the federalist doctrine of implied powers.   Our governmental system was inaugurated under a written constitution which stated in general terms the powers which were to be exercised by the federal government.   Along with the specific grants of power to the national Congress it is further provided that Congress shall make all laws which shall be necessary and proper for carrying into execution the foregoing powers.[3]   On the interpretation of this clause the

---

[1] McCulloch *vs.* Maryland, 4 Wheaton, 316.

[2] Sturges *vs.* Crowninshield, 4 Wheaton, 193.

[3] Art. i, sec. viii.

federalists and the anti-federalists differed greatly. The latter favored a strict construction of the Constitution, holding that only those powers were granted by the Constitution which were absolutely necessary and indispensable to the conduct of the government. The former upheld every means necessary and desirable to carry into effect the powers of the central government, and favored a broad interpretation of the general grants of power given by the Constitution. The issue took a definite form in the policy of Hamilton toward the establishment of a national banking system. The greatest objection raised against the bill presented on the recommendation of Hamilton was on the ground of unconstitutionality. In order to determine the course of the executive, President Washington had asked for a written opinion from his cabinet officers on the constitutionality of the measure.[1] Jefferson denied the right of the general government to pass such a law because no express grant warranted it. The measure was not indispensable to the execution of the powers allotted to the nation and, in his judgment, the right to enact such legislation remained by the Constitution exclusively with the states.[2]

Hamilton argued for the constitutionality of the proposed law and formulated in his opinion the doctrine of implied powers which was later developed very forcibly by Marshall. He regarded the powers granted the central government as expressed and implied, the latter being as effectually delegated as the former. The implied powers were defined as the instrument or means of carrying into effect the specified powers. These implied powers included those means which were needful, requisite, incidental or

[1] Lodge, *The Works of Alexander Hamilton*, ii, pp. 443, 444.

[2] *Works of Jefferson*, vi, p. 197, *et seq.*

conducive to the exercise of any express power. The criterion of constitutionality was then given as the end to which the measure related as a mean. If the end be clearly comprehended within any of the specified powers, and if the measure has an obvious relation to that end, if it is not forbidden by any particular provision of the Constitution, it may safely be deemed to come within the compass of the national authority.[1]

McCulloch vs. Maryland. Hamilton's plan for a bank was adopted in spite of constitutional objections. In 1819 a contest arose over a second bank act in which the whole situation was presented to the Supreme Court for consideration, in the case of McCulloch *vs.* Maryland.[2] On the 11th of February, 1818, the general assembly of Maryland passed an act [3] to impose a tax on all banks or branches thereof in the state of Maryland not chartered by the legislature. As a result of the attempt to execute this law against a branch of the national bank in Baltimore the issue was brought on appeal to the federal Supreme Court. The counsel for the state argued that the bank of the United States was not necessary or indispensable to the carrying on of the operations of the federal government; that the Constitution did not emanate from the people, but as the act of sovereign and independent states; that the acts of Congress chartering and protecting the bank of the United States were not warranted by the Constitution. The states of the Union, it is claimed, have not surrendered themselves, in this manner, by implication, to the Congress of the United States and to such corporations as Congress may create. Corporations not chartered by the state, wholly exempt from taxation, are utterly at variance with

---

[1] *Works of Hamilton, op. cit.,* pp. 444-493.

[2] 4 Wheaton, 316.   [3] *Ibid.,* 320-322.

every principle of government of the United States. The national act is characterized as an overwhelming invasion of state sovereignty not warranted by any express grant from the Constitution.[1] " The federal government is to hold a power by implication and ingenious inference from general words in the Constitution, which it can hardly be believed would have been suffered in an express grant." [2] In answer to the argument that the state would be likely to abuse the power if the right to tax were granted, are placed the propositions, first, that if the states have the power this court cannot take it from them through the fear that they may abuse it; secondly, that the fear of abuse applies just as effectually against permitting an absolute authority in the general government as in permitting a certain degree of control in the states.[3]

Chief Justice Marshall prepared one of the most elaborate opinions of his long judicial career. He regarded the issue raised as a most vital one to the constitutional system of the country, and believed that " it must be decided peacefully, or remain the source of hostile legislation, perhaps hostility of a still more serious nature; and if it is to be so decided, by this tribunal alone can the decision be made. On the Supreme Court of the United States has the Constitution of our country devolved this important duty." [4] Because of the long acceptance of the national bank acts, both by the legislative and by the judicial departments, he thought the acts ought not to be lightly set aside. He reasoned that

If any one proposition could command the universal assent

---

[1] 4 Wheaton, 337.   [2] *Ibid.*, 345.
[3] *Ibid.*, 348.   [4] *Ibid.*, 400, 401.

of mankind, we might expect it would be this—that the government of the Union, though limited in its powers, is supreme within its sphere of action. This would seem to result necessarily from its nature. It is the government of all; its powers are delegated by all; it represents all; and acts for all. Though any one state may be willing to control its operations, no state is willing to allow others to control them. The nation, on those subjects on which it can act, must necessarily bind its component parts.[1]

The government is acknowledged by all to be one of enumerated powers. But questions respecting the extent of the powers actually granted are perpetually arising and will probably continue to arise as long as our system shall exist.

We think the sound construction of the Constitution must allow to the national legislature that discretion, with respect to the means by which the powers it confers are to be carried into execution, which will enable that body to perform the high duties assigned to it, in the manner most beneficial to the people. Let the end be legitimate, let it be within the scope of the Constitution, and all means which are appropriate, which are plainly adapted to that end, which are not prohibited, but which consist with the letter and spirit of the Constitution, are constitutional.[2]

Although the Chief Justice regularly insisted that the government of the United States was one of enumerated powers and that those powers not granted were denied, he used language which indicated that he was willing to allow a very wide latitude in choice of means by the legislative authority. " But where the law is not prohibited, and is really calculated to effect any of the objects entrusted to the

---

[1] 4 Wheaton, 405.

[2] *Ibid.*, 421; *cf. supra*, p. 79, opinion of Hamilton.

government, to undertake here to enquire into the degree of its necessity, would be to pass the line which circumscribes the judicial department, and to tread on legislative ground. This court disclaims any pretension to such a power." [1] That such a construction of the Constitution should be preferred as would render its operations extremely difficult, hazardous and expensive, seemed to him incredible. He deplored the baneful influence of the narrow construction of the Constitution supported by the state and held out the absolute impracticability of maintaining the central government on such a restricted basis. [2]

The national banking system was upheld, the state was prohibited from taxing this corporation of the United States, and it was declared that the national government should not be confined to the execution of the powers strictly enumerated in the Constitution. Marshall pleaded for a " natural " interpretation of the words of the Constitution. In Gibbons *vs.* Ogden he argued

If they contend for that narrow construction which, in support of some theory not to be found in the Constitution, would deny to the government those powers which the words of the grant as usually understood, import, and which are consistent with the general views and objects of the instrument; for that narrow construction which would cripple the government, and render it unequal to the objects for which it is declared to be instituted, and to which the powers given, as fairly understood, render it competent; then we cannot perceive the propriety of this construction, nor adopt it as the rule by which the Constitution is to be expounded. [3]

Powerful and ingenious minds, taking as postulates, that the powers expressly granted to the government of the Union

[1] 4 Wheaton, 423.   [2] *Ibid.,* 417, 418.
[3] 9 Wheaton, 188.

are to be contracted by construction into the narrowest possible compass, and that the original powers of the states are retained if any possible construction will retain them, may, by a course of well digested, but refined and metaphysical reasoning, founded on these premises, explain away the Constitution of our country, and leave it, a magnificent structure, indeed, to look at, but totally unfit for use. They may so entangle and perplex the understanding. as to obscure principles which were before thought quite plain, and induce doubts where, if the mind were to pursue its own course, none would be perceived. In such a case, it is particularly necessary to recur to safe and fundamental principles to sustain those principles, and when sustained, to make them the test of arguments to be examined.[1]

[1] 9 Wheaton, 222.

CHAPTER IV

CONFLICTS OVER THE EXTENSION OF JUDICIAL AUTHORITY

1. Resistance from the States

Contest with Pennsylvania. The Supreme Court had scarcely begun to exercise the wide powers claimed under the doctrines advanced by Marshall before the states were engaged in a series of conflicts with the federal authorities. A most determined resistance was encountered in Pennsylvania in the attempt of the federal Supreme Court to affirm a decision adverse to the state in the case of the Sloop Active.[1] The case had been decided against the state by the Committee on Appeals in Congress, on December 15th, 1778, but the legislature of the state refused to admit that

[1] The Brigantine Convention fitted out by authority of the state of Pennsylvania succeeded in capturing the Sloop Active. The prize was brought before the court of admiralty of the state, which had been organized in accordance with the recommendation of Congress. A trial was conducted before a jury according to the law of the state and a division of the cargo determined upon. From this judgment Gideon Olmstead and several other seamen entered an appeal. The Committee of Appeals in cases of capture re-examined the whole case, set aside the verdict of the jury, and decreed that the proceeds be returned to Olmstead and his fellow seamen. For more than thirty years this judgment had been successfully resisted by the authorities of Pennsylvania on the ground that the Court of Appeals had no right to examine or control the verdict of the jury. For history of case from standpoint of the United States see United States *vs.* Peters, 5 Cranch, 115, *et seq.* For the state see *American State Papers*, Miscellaneous ii, pp. 2-7; *Annals of Congress*, 11 Congress, second session, appendix, pp. 2253-2269.

the Committee had jurisdiction and as a result resisted the enforcement of the decree. The contest was allowed to lapse until 1809 when the issue was placed in the hands of the Supreme Court where the earlier decision of the congressional court was affirmed. Chief Justice Marshall in one of his most characteristic decisions, applied the principles announced in earlier cases, and gave the authorities of the state a severe rebuke. The Chief Justice found that an act of the state required the governor to use any means which he might think necessary to protect the rights of the state and to insure the person and property of the litigants against any process whatever, issued from a federal court.[1] After stating the facts, Justice Marshall declared:

If the legislatures of the several states may, at will, annul the judgments of the courts of the United States, and destroy the rights acquired under those judgments, the Constitution itself becomes a solemn mockery; and the nation is deprived of the means of enforcing its laws by the instrumentality of its own tribunals. So fatal a result must be deprecated by all; and the people of Pennsylvania, not less than the citizens of every other state, must feel a deep interest in resisting principles so destructive of the Union and in averting consequences so fatal to themselves.[2]

It was emphatically maintained that the ultimate right to determine the jurisdiction of the courts of the Union was not placed by the Constitution in the several legislatures but in the Supreme Court of the United States. Consequently it was asserted that the state of Pennsylvania could claim no constitutional right to resist the legal process which might be directed from the Supreme Court.[3]

[1] United States *vs.* Peters, 5 Cranch, 135, 136.
[2] *Ibid.*, 136.   [3] *Ibid.*, 141.

When the decree of the federal court was issued, an act of the Pennsylvania legislature provided that the governor should call out the militia to prevent the enforcement of the judgment.[1] On account of this resistance, the order was made returnable at the next term of court. In the meantime President Madison was asked to intervene on behalf of the state. His reply that " the executive of the United States is not only unauthorized to prevent the execution of a decree sanctioned by the Supreme Court of the United States, but is especially enjoined by statute to carry into effect any such decree where opposition may be made to it," [2] served as a very positive warning to the state authorities. They realized that the state must either submit to the judicial decree or resist the federal government by force of arms. Submission was turned to humiliation, however, when the decree was not only executed but the state officers were also tried for forcibly obstructing the execution of the laws of the nation and were sentenced to fine and imprisonment.[3] The fact that the sentence was remitted by the President, because of his belief that the men had acted under a mistaken sense of duty, did not serve to allay the sense of humiliation which the state had suffered. The resolutions adopted during the time that the marshal delayed in serving his writ shows that the absence of a clear statement in the Constitution regarding the authority to give a final interpretation of the laws had been fully impressed upon a majority of the Pennsylvania assembly.

In a report submitted to the Senate, June 11th, 1809, the legislature of the state claimed that " in resisting encroach-

[1] United States *vs.* Peters, 5 Cranch, 115.

[2] *Works of Madison,* ii, pp. 438, 439.

[3] See Pamphlet, " Trial of General Bright in the Circuit Court of the United States," Philadelphia, 1809.

ments on their rights they are not acting in the spirit of hostility to the legitimate powers of the United States Court, but are actuated by a disposition to compromise, and to guard against future collisions by an amendment to the Constitution." [1] After reviewing the history of the case and attempting to vindicate the policy pursued they submitted a series of resolutions. " It is to be lamented," one resolution reads, " that no provision is made in the Constitution for determining disputes between the general and state governments by an impartial tribunal." [2] It was further resolved, " that from the construction which the United States courts give to their powers, the harmony of the states, if they resist encroachments on their rights, will frequently be interrupted; and if to prevent this evil, they should, on all occasions yield to stretches of power, the reserved rights of the states will depend on the arbitrary power of the courts." [3] The authorities of the state feared that the acceptance of the principle announced by the court would mean the ultimate destruction of the federal nature of our government. They could not accept the idea that the federal government was to be the sole judge of the extent of its own powers, particularly if the courts were to set aside state laws as freely as the laws of the national congress. At the same time the legislature of the state suggested an amendment to be submitted to the states, favoring the establishment of an impartial tribunal to arbitrate difficulties between the state and federal governments.

The recommendation of Pennsylvania was rejected in notices of disapproval from a majority of the states.[4]

---

[1] *American State Papers*, Mis., ii, p. 2.   [2] *Ibid.*, p. 6.   [3] *Ibid.*, p. 6.

[4] See *Journal of Senate of Pennsylvania, 1809-10* for typical replies from the states, New Hampshire, p. 74; Vermont, p. 90; North Carolina, pp. 166, 167.

Virginia adopted an elaborate reply in which it was claimed that the suggestion of Pennsylvania for the establishment of an impartial tribunal to arbitrate between state and nation was uncalled for, because " a tribunal is already provided by the Constitution of the United States, to wit; the Supreme Court, more eminently qualified from their habits and duties, from the mode of their selection and from the tenor of their offices, than any other tribunal which could be erected." [1]   In the face of this reply Virginia could not hope for much assurance of support when in the next few years she found herself in a similar contest over the appellate jurisdiction of the court whose ability, wisdom and impartiality had been lauded so highly.

Contest with Virginia.   When the court of appeals in Virginia, in 1813, declared that the appellate power of the Supreme Court of the United States did not extend to the highest court of the state under a sound construction of the Constitution of the United States, and resisted the exercise of authority over the state by a federal tribunal, the Supreme Court in the powerful opinion of Justice Story upheld the jurisdiction of the courts of the Union by reasoning which was thoroughly national. [2]   After paying a high tribute of respect to the authority of the state court which was under review, Justice Story proceeded with federal doctrine as follows : " the Constitution of the United States was ordained and established, not by the states in their sovereign capacities, but emphatically, as the preamble of the Constitution declares, by the people of the United States." [3]   The people had a right to make the power of the state governments subordinate to those of the nation,

---

[1] Acts of General Assembly of Virginia, 1809-10, p. 102.

[2] Martin *vs.* Hunter's Lessee, 1 Wheaton, 304.

[3] 1 Wheaton, 324.

and this right they have exercised in numerous instances as may be seen by reference to the provisions of the Constitution. Part of the authority surrendered by becoming members of the federal compact was the privilege of determining the final validity of laws which were in conflict with the federal Constitution.[1] Story found that the argument was advanced that "an appellate jurisdiction over state courts is inconsistent with the genius of our governments, and the spirit of the Constitution, that the latter was never designed to act upon state sovereignties, but only upon the people and that if the power exists, it will materially impair the sovereignty of the states and the independence of their courts."[2] In reply he asserted very positively:

It is a mistake that the Constitution was not designed to operate upon states, in their corporate capacity. It is crowded with provisions which restrain or annul the sovereignty of the states in some of the highest branches of their prerogatives. . . . When, therefore, the states are stripped of some of the highest attributes of sovereignty, and the same are given to the United States; when the legislatures of the states are, in some respects under the control of Congress, and in every case are, under the Constitution, bound by the paramount authority of the United States; it is certainly difficult to support the argument that the appellate power over the decisions of state courts is contrary to the genius of our institutions. The courts of the United States can without question, review the executive and legislative authorities of the states, and if they are found to be contrary to the Constitution may declare them to be of no legal validity. Surely the exercise of the same right over judicial tribunals is not a higher or more dangerous act of sovereign power.[3]

---

[1] 1 Wheaton, 325-7.   [2] *Ibid.*, 342.   [3] *Ibid.*, 342, 343.

That no such power as that claimed by the Supreme Court was expressly granted by the Constitution, was a consideration which deserved some attention. One fact alone, Justice Story thought, ought to settle the issue regardless of any grant, that is, the necessity of a uniformity of decisions relative to the Constitution of the United States.[1] This necessity along with the fact that such authority had been regularly exercised by the federal courts ought to settle the question finally and conclusively. Because on an examination of the Constitution, no clause could be found which limited the courts in the exercise of such power, Justice Story observed, " we dare not interpose a limitation where the people have not been disposed to create one." [2]   In the judgment of the court, therefore, the appellate power of the United States extended to cases pending in state courts.

The Supreme Court had now declared itself as a board of arbitration between the federal and state authorities. Following the opinion in the case of Marbury *vs.* Madison, any encroachment on the part of Congress or the President could be prevented by the court; while the opinion of Justice Story was authority for the doctrine that any act of a state—legislative, executive or judicial, even the final voice of the people in the state constitutional convention—could be set aside when considered by the Supreme Court to be in conflict with the provisions of the federal Constitution. The state authorities did not finally submit until the case was re-argued and the decision re-affirmed in the case of Cohens *vs.* Virginia,[3] in 1821, when Chief Justice Marshall clearly followed and enlarged the doctrine earlier announced by Justice Story.

Cohens vs. Virginia. Backed by the doctrine of the

---

[1] 1 Wheaton, 346, 348.   [2] *Ibid.*, 350.
[3] 6 Wheaton, 264.

eleventh amendment that a state may not be sued, Virginia refused to execute an act of Congress, but instead executed one of the acts of its own legislature and claimed that neither the Supreme Court nor any federal power had the right to interfere. The state authorities asserted the right to accept or reject acts of the national Congress. On an appeal to the Supreme Court in which the whole issue was again raised, Marshall, delivering the opinion, determined the question in favor of the nation and silenced for a time those upholding state supremacy:

They maintain, that the nation does not possess a department capable of restraining peaceably, and by authority of law, any attempts which may be made, by a part, against the legitimate powers of the whole; and that the government is reduced to the alternative of submitting to such attempts, or of resisting them by force. They maintain that the Constitution of the United States has provided no tribunal for the final construction of itself, or of the laws or treaties of the nation; but that this power may be exercised in the last resort by the courts of every state in the Union.[1]

The Chief Justice noted that the Constitution declares the laws, treaties, and public acts of the United States to be the supreme law of the land and that the judges in every state shall be bound thereby, anything in the Constitution or laws of any state to the contrary notwithstanding.[2] " This is the authoritative language of the American people; and, if gentlemen please, of the American States . . . The general government though limited in its objects is supreme with respect to these objects. This principle is a part of the Constitution and if there is anyone who denies its necessity no one can deny its authority." [3]   Though a sovereign

[1] 6 Wheaton, 377.   [2] Art. vi, sec. 2.   [3] 6 Wheaton, 381.

and independent state may not be sued without its consent, such liability to suit is a portion of sovereignty that may be surrendered. The judicial department is authorized to decide all cases of every description, arising under the Constitution or laws of the United States. From this general grant of jurisdiction, no exception is made of those cases in which a state may be a party. " We think," Marshall affirmed, " that a case arising under the Constitution or laws of the United States is cognizable in the courts of the Union whoever may be the parties to the case." [1]

In the judgment of Marshall, the necessity or reasonableness of the power to be exercised by the federal courts was not to be regarded as conclusive, though this consideration should not be overlooked when the principles of the Constitution were to be restricted for the purpose of destroying the instrument itself. The mischievous consequences of the construction claimed on the part of Virginia must, he thought, be given great consideration. In many states the judges were dependent for office and salary on the will of the legislature and could not therefore maintain that independence necessary for the determination of constitutional questions.[2] The Constitution was framed for ages to come and was designed to approach immortality as nearly as human institutions could approach it, hence the necessity for fixed, uniform principles of interpretation.[3] On the dangers of dissolution, which were graphically depicted by the counsel for the state, Marshall observed that " whenever hostility to the existing system shall become universal, it will be also irresistible. The people made the Constitution, and the people can unmake it. It is the creature of their will. But this supreme and irresistible power to make and

---

[1] 6 Wheaton, 383.   [2] Ibid., 385-387.
[3] Ibid., 387.

unmake resides in the whole body of the people." [1]   The Chief Justice closed the subject with this warning: " the attempt of any of the parts to exercise it is usurpation, and ought to be repelled by those to whom the people have delegated the power of repelling it." [2]   When taking into account the number of state governments, the conclusion was reached that twenty independent courts of final jurisdiction over the same causes arising under the same laws was a hydra in government, from which nothing but contradictions and confusion could proceed.   Such a construction would reduce to a nullity almost the entire Constitution and must in the consideration of that instrument be held untenable. [3]

Virginia had lost her case and the national government had gained a decisive victory, for the eleventh amendment, adopted to protect state authority, was reduced by interpretation to a very insecure basis for the maintenance of state independence.

Jefferson's Objections.   The most formidable opponent of Marshall and the federal principles of interpretation adopted by the Supreme Court, ex-President Jefferson, gave a final and comprehensive opinion on the case which Virginia had lost.   In a letter to William Johnson in June, 1823, Jefferson reviewed the history of the contest between the federalists and antifederalists.   Regarding the request to examine the question whether the Supreme Court had advanced beyond its constitutional limits, he replied, that age disqualified him for the task and that this examination had already been very well done.   He then referred to certain papers which appeared in the *Enquirer* prepared by Judge Roane under the name of Algernon Sydney: [4]

[1] 6 Wheaton, 389.   [2] *Ibid.*, 389.   [3] *Ibid.*, 415, 416.
[4] *Works of Jefferson*, xii, pp. 252-259.

I considered these papers maturely as they came out, and confess that they appeared to me to pulverize every word which had been delivered by Judge Marshall, of the extra-judicial part of his opinion; and all was extra-judicial, except the decision that the act of Congress had not purported to give to the corporation of Washington the authority claimed by their lottery law, of controlling the laws of the states within the states themselves. But unable to claim that case he could not let it go entirely, but went on gratuitously to prove, that notwithstanding the eleventh amendment, a state could be brought as a defendant to the bar of his court; and again, that Congress might authorize a corporation of its territory to exercise legislation within a state, and paramount to the laws of that state.[1]

This doctrine of Marshall, Jefferson thought, " was so completely refuted by Roane, that if he can be answered, I surrender human reason as a vain and useless faculty given to bewilder and not to guide us." [2]   This practice of Judge Marshall, " of travelling out of his case to prescribe what the law would be in a moot case not before the court," was regarded as very irregular and censurable.[3] To bear out these criticisms Marbury *vs.* Madison was cited.   In this case the court determined at once, that being an original process, they did not have cognizance of it, and therefore the question before them was ended.   But the Chief Justice went on to lay down what the law would be, if they had jurisdiction over the case.   " The object was clearly to instruct any other court having the jurisdiction what they should do if Marbury should apply to them." [4]   Although the court could not issue a mandamus to the President or legislature, said Jefferson, " this case of Marbury *vs.* Madison is continually cited by bench and bar as if it were settled law."

[1] Works, *op. cit.*, p. 255.   [2] *Ibid.*, p. 255.
[3] *Ibid.*, p. 256.   [4] *Ibid.*, pp. 256, 257.

As a partial remedy for the danger with which Jefferson thought this practice was replete, he advocated an amendment that each judge should give his individual opinion on all issues raising the constitutionality of laws.   In the last reference to this practice he expressed the opinion that there was more hostility to the federal judiciary than to any other organ of the government.[1]   He did not live to see the triumph of those radical democratic ideas which led to a decided change of attitude on the part of the judiciary in dealing with federal and state legislation.

In Ohio.   As early as 1808 a strong sentiment was aroused against a few judges who ventured to declare a state law unconstitutional.   A part of an act of the legislature defining the duties of justices of the peace was held to be repugnant to the Constitution of the United States and the constitution of the state of Ohio, and therefore null and void.[2]   The clamor and abuse of the judges were not affected by the fact that a majority of the members of the supreme court of the state favored the decision.   At the session of the legislature for 1807-1808 steps were taken to impeach Judge Pease, who first refused to enforce the law, and Justice Tod, one of the Supreme Court justices. The decisions of the courts were denounced as an assault upon the wisdom and dignity as well as the supremacy of the legislature.   But as in the other cases of impeachment the trial resulted in the acquittal of both judges.

Resistance to the act establishing a national bank continued in Ohio even after the settlement of the controversy in Maryland and the complete victory of the national au-

[1] *Works, op. cit.,* p. 280.

[2] Sketch of Hon. Calvin Pease, Western Law Monthly, v, p. 3, June, 1863, quoted in Cooley, *Constitutional Limitations* (seventh edition) pp. 229, 230.

thorities there. On February 8th, 1819, the general assembly of Ohio passed a law levying a tax of $50,000 on each branch of the bank of the United States established in the state. The tax was meant to be prohibitive and the amounts were to be speedily collected. Two branches refused to pay the tax and the state authorities forcibly seized the sum of $100,000 from one of the banks. Suits were begun and criminal prosecutions instituted against the officers of the state, and while the suits were under consideration the general assembly met. Reports and resolutions were drawn up and sent to the Senate and House of Representatives. At the same time an act was passed to withdraw from the bank of the United States the protection of the laws of the state.[1] On an appeal to the Supreme Court of the United States the former decision was re-affirmed and the state laws declared null and void.[2]

In a report submitted to Congress from the state, the objection was raised that the state was reduced to the level of an ordinary citizen and made answerable in inferior tribunals. As the auditor of the state was sued it was contended that, in everything but name, the state was the actual defendant.[3] It was evident that the principle of the proceeding secured to the federal tribunals every power supposed to be taken from them by the eleventh amendment.[4] " The committee are aware of the doctrine that the federal courts are exclusively vested with jurisdiction to declare, in the last resort, the true interpretation of the Constitution of the United States. To this doctrine in the latitude contended for they can never give their consent." [5]

[1] Ames, *State Documents on Federal Relations*, pp. 93, 94.

[2] Osborne *vs.* the United States, 9 Wheaton, 738.

[3] *Senate Documents*, 16 Congress, 2nd Session xii, no. 72, pp. 6, 7, 8.

[4] *Ibid.*, p. 10.   [5] *Ibid.*, p. 11.

The report further stated that after the adoption of the
eleventh amendment the courts of the United States ceased
to be the proper constitutional tribunals to investigate and
determine the power and authority of the states under the
Constitution of the United States. Marbury *vs.* Madison
and Fletcher *vs.* Peck were cited as cases wherein a decision
of the Supreme Court of the United States was not conclusive on great questions of political rights and political
powers.[1]

The propositions of Chief Justice Marshall in the decision of McCulloch *vs.* Maryland were then summarized and
respectively denied. As a result of this decision the committee thought that " the government of the Union may and
undoubtedly will, progressively draw all the powers of the
government into the vortex of its authority." [2]   The report
continued :

It is important to glance at the train of implications with
which this doctrine is connected. The power to create the
bank implies the power to preserve it. This power to create,
is, itself, derived by implication . . . and the power to
preserve implies a choice in selecting the means of preservation, and upon the doctrine of the court, all these powers are
supreme, to the operation of which, the constitutions and laws
of the states can oppose no obstacle. It is certainly difficult
to see the point where these implications terminate or to
name the power which they leave to the states unimpaired.[3]

The report closed with a series of resolutions denying
federal jurisdiction over the state in the case under consideration and protesting against the doctrine " that the
political rights of the separate states that compose the
American Union and their powers as sovereign states, may

[1] *Senate Documents, op. cit.,* pp. 17, 18.
[2] *Ibid.,* p. 22.   [3] *Ibid.,* p. 25.

be settled and determined in the Supreme Court of the United States." [1]

In Kentucky. The resistance to the doctrine of judicial nullification was maintained with even greater ardor in Kentucky. Although the right had been asserted by a Kentucky court in 1801,[2] the opposition to the practice did not result in any positive action until the decision was rendered by Judge Clark, in 1822, on the validity of the relief laws. The session of the Kentucky legislature which met in 1820 passed a series of laws providing an easy method for the release of obligations which were burdening the debtor class of the state. One of these laws was contested before Judge Clark on the ground that it was in violation of the Constitution of the United States and the constitution of the state. Judge Clark granted an order which was intended as a refusal to enforce the law and stated the reasons for his decision.[3]

When this decision became known the Kentucky house of representatives which was then in session resolved that,

Whereas this house is informed that Judge James Clark has . . . given a decision in contravention of the laws of this commonwealth, called the endorsement and replevin laws, and therein grossly transcended his judicial authority and disregarded the constitutional powers of the legislature of this commonwealth : Therefore, Resolved that a committee be appointed to inquire into the decision of the said Judge, and report thereon to this house.[4]

In a few days the chairman, Mr. Slaughter, reported for

---

[1] *Senate Documents, op. cit.,* p. 34.
[2] Stidger *vs.* Rogers, Kentucky Decisions, 52.
[3] Williams *vs.* Blair, *Niles Register,* xxiii, supplement, p. 153.
[4] Niles, *op. cit.,* p. 155.

the committee. The principles and doctrines of Judge Clark's opinion were denounced as

Incompatible with the constitutional powers of the legislative department of this government, subversive of the best interests of the people, and calculated in their consequences to disturb the tranquillity of the country, and to shake the public confidence in the institutions and measures of the government, called for by the condition and the necessities of the people. That the judicial department has a power, beyond control, to defeat the general policy of the state, deliberately adopted by the representatives of the people, within the pale of their authority is a position which your committee are not prepared to admit.[1]

The committee recommended the removal of Judge Clark from office and proceedings toward impeachment were immediately instituted. Several days were granted to the Judge to file an answer and a vote was then taken which resulted in acquittal, 59, less than the necessary two-thirds, voting in favor and 35 against the motion. The governor in his message of the following year approved the laws and also denounced the courts for refusing to enforce the legislative acts.[2] In the same year, the court of appeals upheld the decision of the lower court [3] with the result that the contest was continued in a political fight at the polls. The people of the state were separated into two distinct organizations, the " old court party " and the " new court party." The election resulted in a complete victory for the " new court party " and the issue gradually passed out of Kentucky politics.[4]

Green vs. Biddle. While this contest was engaging the

[1] Niles, *op. cit.*, p. 155.   [2] *Ibid.*, p. 156.
[3] Lapsley *vs.* Breashear, 4 Litt. *Kentucky Reports*, p. 47.
[4] Collins, *History of Kentucky*, i, p. 218, *et seq.*

attention of the state authorities, the opposition to the judiciary was thoroughly aroused over a decision of the federal Supreme Court. An act of the state of Kentucky concerning the title to certain land grants which involved an agreement with the state of Virginia, was held to be repugnant to the Constitution of the United States as in violation of a contract between the two states.[1] The legislature of the state adopted a long report with a separate series of resolutions relative to the above decisions and submitted a remonstrance to Congress.[2] A decided protest was entered against what was termed "the erroneous, injurious and degrading doctrines of the opinion of the Supreme Court of the United States."[3]

On account of the fact that three justices were absent at the time the opinion was rendered in the federal court, and only three out of the four present concurred in the decision, a recommendation was made that no constitutional question relating to the validity of laws of Congress or of the laws of the states should be determined unless two-thirds of the members of the court concurred in the decision. In the report to Congress, the state maintained, that

It is the principle which that decision establishes at which they shudder, and with which they can never be reconciled. The people of Kentucky . . . can bear anything but degradation and disfranchisement. They cannot bear to be construed out of their right of self-government; they value their freedom above everything else and are as little inclined to be reasoned out of it, as they would be to surrender it to foreign force.[4]

[1] Green *vs.* Biddle, 8 Wheaton, 1.
[2] For history of this conflict, see Ames, *op. cit.*, pp. 17-23.
[3] *Ibid.*, p. 19.
[4] *Senate Documents*, 18 Congress, 1st session, iv, no. 69, p. 8.

On the failure of Congress to grant the relief desired by the state authorities, the issue was again brought before the legislature in 1825 by a message from the governor. The house of representatives sent an inquiry to the governor asking information regarding the proper procedure " to refuse obedience to the decisions and mandates of the Supreme Court of the United States, considered erroneous and unconstitutional, and whether, in the opinion of the executive, it may be advisable to call forth the physical power of the state to resist the execution of the decisions of the court, or in what manner the mandate of said court should be met by disobedience." [1]   As the governor was not inclined to assume the responsibility of the use of physical force, a feeble resistance was continued until 1831 when a second decision of the Supreme Court was accepted as final by the state authorities. [2]

On account of the conflicts with the states from 1809 to 1830, numerous measures were introduced in the Senate and House of Representatives with the intention of restricting the powers and jurisdiction of the federal courts, but all were dropped either in committee or on the floor of Congress.   A series of amendments suggested by the states had suffered a similar fate.   The authority of the court, however, was soon to suffer from the particularist tendencies of the democratic party.   A discussion of these tendencies may well be prefaced by the thorough analysis of the right of judicial nullification by Justice Gibson of Pennsylvania.

2. The dissenting opinion of Justice Gibson of Pennsylvania

The most elaborate attack upon the doctrine of judicial nullification was that embodied in the dissenting opinion of Justice Gibson in the case of Eakin *vs.* Raub in the Supreme

[1] Niles, xxix, pp. 228, 229.

[2] Hawkins *vs.* Barney's Lessees, 5 Peters, 457.

Court of Pennsylvania.[1] The argument dealt with a state statute and the decision of the highest court of the state, but the reasoning of Justice Gibson and his criticisms applied with equal force to the practice announced by the federal courts.

The case arose out of an action of ejectment. The principal question in the case was, whether the plaintiffs, who resided in Ireland, were barred from bringing suit as a result of the act of limitations passed March 26th, 1785 and a supplement thereto passed March 15th, 1815. According to the construction of the court, no constitutional question was involved but since some doubts, relative to the judicial right to set aside legislative acts, were raised in argument, Chief Justice Tilghman in his opinion, held that,

I adhere to the opinion which I have frequently expressed that when a judge is convinced, beyond doubt, that an act has been passed in violation of the constitution, he is bound to declare it void, by his oath, by his duty to the party who has brought the cause before him, and to the people, the only source of legitimate power, who, when they formed the constitution of the state, expressly declared that certain things were excepted out of the general powers of government and should forever remain inviolate. . . . Upon this subject I have ever entertained but one opinion, which has been strengthened by reflection, and fortified by the concurring sentiments of the Supreme Court of the United States, as well as of lawyers, judges, and statesmen of the highest standing in all parts of the United States of America.[2]

In a dissenting opinion Justice Gibson was impelled by the remarks of the Chief Justice to express his views on the abstract right of the judiciary to declare legislative acts

[1] 12 Sergeant and Rawles, *Pennsylvania Reports,* 330.
[2] *Ibid.,* 339, 340.

void. After making a distinction between acts that were regarded as being repugnant to the constitution of a particular state and acts repugnant to the Constitution of the United States, the Chief Justice remarked: " I am aware, that a right to declare all unconstitutional acts void, without distinction as to either constitution, is generally held as a professional dogma; but, I apprehend rather as a matter of faith than of reason. I admit that I once embraced the same doctrine, but without examination, and I shall therefore state the arguments that impelled me to abandon it, with great respect for those by whom it is still maintained." [1] No judge except Chief Justice Marshall in Marbury *vs.* Madison had ventured to discuss the right in question, although the judiciary had all along claimed the privilege of doing so. The opinion of Judge Patterson, in Vanhorne *vs.* Dorrance,[2] was characterized as abounding in beautiful figures and metaphorical illustration without a real basis in argument. It was claimed that in the determination of this question, precedents ought to count for absolutely nothing. " The Constitution is a collection of fundamental laws, not to be departed from in practice nor altered by judicial decision. . . . Instead, therefore, of resting on the fact that the right in question has universally been assumed by the American courts, the judge who asserts it ought to be prepared to maintain it on the principle of the Constitution." [3]

Judicial powers divided into political and civil.[4] In this

---

[1] 12 Sergeant and Rawles, 345, 346.

[2] 2 Dallas, 307.　　　　　　　　　[3] 12 S. and R., 346.

[4] *Ibid.,* 356; the topical headings and the arrangement of arguments are my own. The opinion has been condensed except in certain parts where the language of Justice Gibson is used for the sake of clearness and emphasis.

country, argues Justice Gibson, it is found that the powers
of the judiciary are divisible into those that are political
and those that are purely civil. A political power is one
by which one organ of government controls another or ex-
erts an influence over its acts. The political powers of
the judiciary are extraordinary and are such as are derived, by direct grant, from the common fountain of all
political power. The civil powers, however, are the ordinary functions and exist independently of any supposed grant
in the constitution. Justice Gibson claims that where a
government exists by virtue of a written constitution the
judiciary does not necessarily derive any other than its ordinary and appropriate powers.[1] Our judiciary is constructed on the principles of common law, and in adopting
any organ or instrument of common law, we take it with
just such powers as were incident to it at common law, except where they are expressly or by necessary implication
abridged or enlarged in the act of adoption. On this principle the powers of the judiciary have to do with the judicial execution of the municipal law, or, with the administration of distributive justice, without extending to anything of a political cast whatever. Dr. Paley is then quoted
with approval to the effect that the judiciary must be considered as a part of the executive, and therefore subordinate to the legislature, the depository of the whole sovereignty of the state.[2] This feature of the opinion is concluded with these remarks:

It will be conceded then, that the ordinary and essential powers
of the judiciary do not extend to the annulling of an act of
the legislature. Nor can the inference to be drawn from this,
be evaded by saying that in England the constitution, resting

[1] 12 S. and R., 346.   [2] *Ibid.,* 346.

in principles consecrated by time, and not in an actual written compact, and being subject to alteration by the very act of the legislature, there is consequently no separate and distinct criterion by which the question of constitutionality may be determined; for it does not follow that because we have such a criterion, the application of it belongs to the judiciary. I take it, therefore, that the power in question does not necessarily arise from the judiciary being established by a written constitution, but that this organ can claim, on account of that circumstance, no powers that do not belong to it at the common law; and that, whatever may have been the cause of the limitation of its jurisdiction originally, it can exercise no power of supervision over the legislature, without producing a direct authority for it in the constitution, either in terms or by irresistible implication from the nature of the government: without which the power must be considered as reserved, along with the other ungranted portions of the sovereignty, for the immediate use of the people.[1]

State laws contrary to the Constitution of the United States. The authority of the judiciary over an act of an assembly or a state constitution which is in conflict with the Constitution, laws or treaties of the United States is directly recognized in the Constitution itself. The states agreed to certain limitations of their own sovereignty in the adoption of the federal Constitution. These limitations were to be made effective against the states through the instrumentality of their judges. The federal Constitution declares that the Constitution and the laws of the United States shall be the supreme law of the land and that the judges in every state shall be bound thereby.[2]

This is a direct grant of a political power, and is positive proof that no state law shall be executed at the expense of the Constitution, laws or treaties of the United

---

[1] 12 S. and R., 347.   [2] Art. vi, sec. 2.

States. The argument that the Constitution applies only when there is no state law on the subject would completely nullify this provision and is therefore inadmissible. No act of the state can directly or indirectly dispense with the federal Constitution and state judges are directed to uphold federal statutes above any of those of the state.

The Constitution likewise provides for appellate jurisdiction in the federal courts over all national laws, under such regulations as Congress may prescribe.[1] Congress has directed that all cases involving the construction of federal laws or treaties may be removed by writ of error to the Supreme Court of the United States. This law, along with a direct constitutional mandate, binds the states to the execution of federal laws.[2]

The constitution a law of superior obligation.[3] As the constitution of the state contains no express grant of the power to nullify state laws, it must therefore be established by implication from the fact that the state constitution is a law of superior obligation; and in case of a conflict an act of the legislature would have to give way to the constitution. This Justice Gibson concedes, but it is a fallacy, he claims, to suppose that a conflict can arise before the judiciary. He defines a constitution as an act of extraordinary legislation, by which the people establish the structure of their government; and a statute, as an act of ordinary legislation, the provisions of which are to be executed by the executive or the judiciary. The constitution, he finds, contains no practical rules for the administration of justice, with which alone the judiciary has to do. It is generally true, that the provisions of a constitution are to be carried into effect immediately by the legislature, and

---

[1] Art. iii, sec. 2.   [2] 12 S. and R., 356, 357.

[3] *Ibid.*, 347.

only mediately, if at all, by the judiciary. In certain specific cases where the provisions of the constitution deal with judicial processes or procedure, the language is directed to the courts and they may well resist any change to the contrary by the legislature. In all other cases, there is no other rule to guide the courts in the interpretation of the law beyond the act of assembly under consideration. The constitution and act of assembly do not furnish conflicting rules applicable to the point before the court; nor is it at all necessary that one or the other should give way.[1]

Power necessary to uphold a written constitution.[2] The argument that such a power in the judiciary is necessary to secure the principles of a written constitution is readily disposed of. The fear that the legislature will become arbitrary, and that constitutions will be thereby rendered useless, calls for a determination of the purpose of a written constitution. Such documents can have no other purpose than to outline certain principles and to affirm definite rights, which are thus brought to the particular attention of the people. Principles of government no longer need depend wholly upon tradition and the vague notions of those in authority. But, Justice Gibson thinks, there is no magic or inherent power in parchment and ink, to protect principles from violation. In the business of government, he believes, a recurrence to first principles is very necessary and for this purpose he regards a written constitution as an instrument of inestimable value. It serves the purpose also of rendering these principles familiar to the mass of the people, and tends to arouse public opinion which is considered as the only effectual safeguard against legislative usurpation. The constitution of Pennsylvania, he finds, has withstood the shocks of strong party excitement for

[1] 12 S. and R., 348.   [2] *Ibid.*, 354, 355.

thirty years, without a single case of the exercise of this right by the judiciary.[1]

Legislative acts ipso facto void. The theory which was generally accepted during the first period of the American government, that legislatures possess no inherent right of legislation but derive all authority from the people in the form of grants in written constitutions, is met by Justice Gibson with equal vigor. On this theory, the constitution fixes the sphere of action of the legislature, and no law can be valid for which power is not granted. The conclusion then follows that acts not warranted by the constitution are not acts of the people and are therefore *ipso facto* void. A law that is *ipso facto* void is regarded as if it never had been and must be entirely ignored. But Justice Gibson thinks that it is an audacious claim to assert that the deliberate and well-matured judgment of one of the regularly constituted departments of government, expressed in the form of acts passed under a strict observance of the principles of the constitution, shall be rejected as *ipso facto* void.[2] All respect is demanded for the acts of the judiciary when a law is declared unconstitutional. The legislature, it is held, must acquiesce even though it may think the construction of the judiciary wrong. This claim rests solely on the ground that the legislature ought to respect the judgment of a co-ordinate department of the government. Why should not the same respect be rendered to the judgment of the legislature? It will not be pretended " that the legislature has not at least an equal right with the judiciary to put a construction on the constitution, nor that either of them is infallible; nor that either ought to be required to surrender its judgment to the other."[3]

Refusal to execute an unconstitutional law. But the

[1] 12 S. and R., 354, 355.   [2] *Ibid.,* 349.   [3] *Ibid.,* 349.

advocates of judicial nullification ask: " do not the judges
do a positive act in violation of the constitution, when
they give effect to an unconstitutional law?" The fallacy of this question lies, says Justice Gibson, in suppos-
ing that the judiciary adopts the acts of legislature; whereas the enactment of law and the interpretation of it are two
separate acts, and as the judiciary is not required to concur in the enactment, neither is it in the breach of the constitution which may be the consequence of the enactment.
The fault is imputable to the legislature and on it the responsibility rests.[1] This argument is regarded as nothing
more than a repetition of the claim that an " unconstitutional law is *ipso facto* void;" since a refusal to enforce a
law can be based only on the right of one department to
assert authority over the other departments.   No such right
is recognized in the branches of the national government,
except in the judiciary.[2]

The oath of judges to support the constitution.   That
the judges are sworn to support the constitution, and are
bound by it as the law of the land, is another argument in
favor of this particular type of judicial review.   In reply,
Justice Gibson observes that if the official duty of a judge
does not comprehend an inquiry into the authority of the
legislature, the oath in support of the constitution gives him
no such special prerogative.   The basis of every argument in favor of the right of the judiciary is found, in last
analysis, to be an assumption of the whole ground in dispute.   Even if the oath of a judge is to secure support of
the constitution in the discharge of his official duty, it can
apply only to the exercise of ordinary judicial powers.
The constitution is intended to furnish a rule of construction where particular interpretation of a law would conflict

[1] 12 S. and R., 354.   [2] *Ibid.,* 351.

with some constitutional provision, and wherever possible such interpretation is to be avoided. The oath was more probably designed to secure the powers of each of the different branches from being usurped by any of the others, such as, to prevent the House of Representatives from erecting itself into a court of justice, or the Supreme Court from attempting to control the legislature. In this view, the oath of the judges may be used with equal force against the right of judiciary. " The official oath, then, relates only to the official conduct of the officer, and does not prove that he ought to stray from the path of his ordinary business to search for violations of duty in the business of others; nor does it, as supposed, define the powers of the officer." [1]

Cases must be free from doubt. The power of nullification is said to be restricted to cases that are free from doubt or difficulty. But Justice Gibson thinks the abstract existence of power cannot depend on the clearness or obscurity of the case in which it is to be exercised; for this question cannot present itself before the existence of the power shall have been determined. No considerations of policy ought to influence the exercise of this right. [2]

The notion of a complication of counterchecks has been carried to an extent, in theory, of which the framers of the Constitution never dreamt. When governmental powers were distributed to the appropriate branches, all things incident to the exercise of these powers were committed to each branch exclusively. The checks upon each department were definitely provided for so as to maintain the essential features of the principle of the separation of powers. Had it been intended to have the judiciary serve as an additional check, the matter would surely not have been left in doubt. The judges would not have been left to stand on the insecure

[1] 12 S. and R., 353.   [2] *Ibid.*, 352, 353.

ground of public opinion as to constructive powers. They would have been placed on the impregnable ground of an express grant, and as a consequence would not have been compelled to resort to the debates in the convention, or the opinion that was generally entertained at the time to uphold the assertion of such remarkable powers.[1] Justice Gibson claims that what he wishes to impress upon the attention particularly is,

The necessity of yielding to the acts of the legislature the same respect that is claimed for the acts of the judiciary. Repugnance to the constitution is not always self-evident; for questions involving the consideration of its existence, require for their solution the most vigorous exertion of the higher faculties of the mind, and conflicts will be inevitable if any branch is to apply the constitution after its own fashion to the acts of all others. I take it, then, the legislature is entitled to all the deference that is due to the judiciary; that its acts are in no case to be treated as ipso facto void, except where they would produce a revolution in the government; and, that, to avoid them, requires the act of some tribunal competent under the constitution, (if any such there be,) to pass on their validity. All that remains, therefore, is to inquire whether the judiciary or the people are that tribunal.[2]

Since the judiciary is not expressly constituted as the judge of constitutionality, it must derive such authority from the reasonableness or fitness of the thing. But as legislation peculiarly involves the consideration of the limitations placed upon the law-making power, and the interpretation of the laws involves only the construction of the laws as enacted, it would seem to follow that the construction of the constitution belongs primarily to the legis-

[1] 12 S. and R., 351, 352.   [2] *Ibid.*, 350.

lature which ought to have the capacity to judge the constitutionality of its own acts.[1]

Power rests with the people to keep legislation within constitutional limits. The concluding arguments of Justice Gibson are as follows:

That the judiciary is of superior rank has never been pretended although it has been said to be co-ordinate. It is not easy, however, to comprehend how the power which gives law to all the rest, can be of no higher rank than the one which receives it. . . . Legislation is essentially an act of sovereign power; but the execution of the laws by instruments that are governed by prescribed rules, and exercise no power of volition, is essentially otherwise. The very definiton of law, which is said to be " a rule of civil conduct prescribed by the supreme power of the state," shows the intrinsic superiority of the legislature. It may be said the power of the legislature, also, is limited by prescribed rules. It is so. But it is, nevertheless, the power of the people, and sovereign as far as it extends. It cannot be said, that the judiciary is co-ordinate merely because it is established by the constitution. . . . Inequality of rank arises not from the manner in which the organ has been constituted, but from its essence and the nature of its functions; and the legislative organ is superior to every other, inasmuch as the power to will and command, is essentially superior to the power to act and obey. It does not follow, then, that every organ created by special provision in the constitution is of equal rank. Both the executive, strictly as such, and the judiciary are subordinate; and an act of superior power exercised by an inferior ought, one would think, to rest on something more solid than implication.[2]

The constitution and the right of the legislature to pass the act, may be in collision but is that a legitimate subject for judicial determination? If it be, the judiciary must be a

[1] 12 S. and R., 350.   [2] *Ibid.*, 350, 351.

peculiar organ to revise the proceedings of the legislature, and to correct its mistakes; and in what part of the constitution are we to look for this proud pre-eminence? Viewing the matter in the opposite direction, what would be thought of an act of assembly in which it should be declared that the Supreme Court had, in a particular case, put a wrong construction on the Constitution of the United States, and that judgment should therefore be reversed? It would doubtless be thought a usurpation of judicial power. But it is by no means clear that to declare a law void which has been enacted according to the forms prescribed in the Constitution is not a usurpation of legislative power. It is an act of sovereignty; and sovereignty and legislative power are said by Sir William Blackstone to be convertible terms. It is the business of the judiciary to interpret the laws, not scan the authority of the lawgiver; and without the latter it cannot take cognizance of a collision between a law and the constitution. So that to affirm that the judiciary has a right to judge of the existence of such collisions, is to take for granted the very thing to be proved.[1]

For these reasons, I am of the opinion that it rests with the people, in whom full and absolute sovereign power resides, to correct abuses in legislation, by instructing their representatives to repeal the obnoxious act. What is wanting to plenary power in the government, is reserved by the people for their own immediate use; and to redress an infringement of their rights in this respect would seem to be an accessory of the power thus reserved. It might, perhaps, have been better to vest the power in the judiciary; as it might be expected that its habits of deliberation, and the aid derived from the arguments of counsel, would more frequently lead to accurate conclusions. On the other hand the judiciary is not infallible; and an error by it would admit of no remedy but a more distinct expression of the public will, through the ex-

[1] 12 S. and R., 348.

traordinary medium of a convention; whereas, an error of the legislature admits of a remedy by an exertion of the same will, in the ordinary exercise of the right of suffrage,—a mode better calculated to attain the end, without popular excitement. It may be said, the people would not notice an error of their representatives. But they would as probably do so as notice an error of the judiciary; and besides it is a postulate in the theory of our government, and the very basis of the super-structure that the people are wise, virtuous and competent to manage their own affairs: and if they are not so, in fact, still every question of this sort must be determined according to the principles of the constitution, as it came from the hands of its framers, and the existence of a defect which was not foreseen, would not justify those who administer the government in applying a corrective in practice which can be provided only by a convention. Long and uninterrupted usage is entitled to respect; and although it cannot change an admitted principle of the constitution, it will go far to settle a question of doubtful right. But although this power has all along been claimed by the state judiciary, it has never been exercised. Austin vs. The University of Pennsylvania (1 Yates, 260) is the only case even apparently to the contrary; but there the act of assembly had been previously repealed. In Vanhorne vs. Dorrance, decided by the circuit court of the United States under similar circumstances, the right is preemptorily asserted, and examples of monstrous violations of the constitution are put in a strong light by way of example; such as taking away the right of jury, the elective franchise, or subverting religious liberty. But any of these would be such a usurpation of the political rights of the citizen as would work a change in the very structure of the government; or, to speak more properly, it would itself be a revolution, which, to counteract, would justify even insurrection,—consequently a judge might lawfully employ every instrument of official resistance within his reach. By this I mean, that while the citizens should resist with pike and gun, the judge might cooperate with *habeas corpus* and *mandamus*. It will be his duty, as a citizen, to throw himself into the breach, and, if it should be necessary, perish there; but this is far from proving the judiciary to be a peculiar organ under the Constitution; to prevent legislative encroachment on the powers reserved by the people; and this is all that I contend that it is not. Indeed, its absolute inadequacy to the object, is conclusive that it never was intended as such by the framers of the constitution, who must have had in view the probable operation of the government in practice.[1]

In this opinion, one argument in favor of the principle of judicial interpretation of legislative acts was frankly admitted, namely, that the laws of the nation were to be supreme and that the laws of the states repugnant to any national law should give way; and that the judiciary was the proper body to determine when there was a conflict between the two grades of law. So much was expressly granted in the words of the Constitution. Every other feature of judicial nullification, especially that practice by which the Supreme Court established the right to set aside laws of Congress and secured a very extensive veto by interpretation on the laws of the states, as well as the practice by which the state courts asserted authority over the general assembly of the state, had been according to the opinion of Chief Justice Gibson developed out of the theories, customs and constructions of the justices, state and federal, since 1780.

Few men of the time realized that the acceptance of one feature of the practice of nullifying legislative acts—the well-recognized fact that the courts of both state and nation were expected to deal with a conflict between a state law and a national law—did not necessarily involve the ac-

[1] 12 S. and R., 355, 356.

ceptance of the other feature of the practice, that a judicial
decision must be regarded as final and authoritative even
above the legislatures of state and nation. The latter however was generally considered as a necessary result of the
former and the difference in importance between the two
propositions was seldom noted. The opinion of Justice
Gibson appears to be the only critical examination of the
whole doctrine by one who was opposed to judicial supremacy on the ground of principle and policy.

In 1845, this opinion was quoted in an argument of counsel before the supreme court of the state. Gibson, who had
been advanced to the position of Chief Justice, remarked,
" I have changed that opinion for two reasons. The late
convention, by their silence, sanctioned the pretensions of
the court to deal freely with the acts of the legislature; and
from experience of the necessity of the case." [1] Another of
those who opposed the American practice of judicial nullification, and one who had very cogently expressed the reasons for his opposition, was compelled to fall in line with
the powerful trend of public opinion in spite of many
misgivings that the nation on this issue was heading in the
wrong direction.

3. American doctrine of Civil Liberty

State after state had stood out against the assertion of
the right of courts to nullify legislative acts. But as no con-
certed action on any given cause could be secured in a majority of the states, while in every case the states unaf-
fected by the particular decision denounced the attitude of
the party concerned, there was no hope of placing an effective curb upon the extension of judicial authority. And
when it is considered that in almost every instance the au-

---

[1] Norris *vs.* Clymer, 2 *Pennsylvania State Reports*, 281.

thority of the state had to submit entirely, without possibility of compromise, it is not strange that in succeeding decades the courts should have felt at liberty to refuse their sanction to legislative enactments. The tendency of the time was decidedly in favor of nationalism. The federalists had always stood for a strong central government. The new democratic-republican party advocated a theory of restriction of governmental powers and inclined toward the doctrine of state rights, but the whole trend of the time tended to make this party itself national. Party leaders seemed to have changed ground completely, until it appeared that all were nationalists. The tide was setting in the direction of a stronger and stronger central government. The center of the whole machinery, it was thought, was the judicial system guided by the principle of judicial control over all departments of government. The success of the whole experiment seemed to hinge upon this feature of the system. The stability of the federal structure was thought to depend upon the unimpaired dignity of the judicial body, which was growing into one of the mightiest of legal tribunals. The theory and practice of the time favored the establishment of the Supreme Court as the guardian and final interpreter of the Constitution of the United States.

The significance of the practice and its influence upon the political system of the United States, were scarcely comprehended in this early period. In the development of this doctrine and its acceptance by the people lies the basis for the fact that the courts in the United States are continually called upon to deal with questions that are purely political and governmental; to enter, partially at least, into the realm of legislation; and to discuss questions of political, economic and social theory. A government based upon a Constitution for all ordinary purposes beyond the reach of a changing and developing public opinion, and a national government limited to the powers expressly granted, might have been unworkable except for the adoption of broad and liberal principles of construction by the court which had declared itself to be the supreme interpreter of law and principles of government. The arguments upholding the opinions of the court were so cogently stated that it soon became a settled conviction that the practice of judicial nullification of legislative acts was necessary to a federal system of government, and that a written constitution demands such a tribunal as our Supreme Court with all the powers which it has been accustomed to exercise.

By 1830, the nation had become accustomed even to the radical form of the doctrine announced by Chief Justice Marshall. The states had one by one engrafted the practice upon their systems of constitutional law [1] and the American government was strongly entrenched in a form very different in one point at least from the governments of ancient and modern times. Every court, local, state or national, began to feel at liberty to question the acts of Congress or of state legislatures, and relied upon the Supreme Court to bear out its interpretation even though the solemn enactment of the representatives of the people in the Senate and House of Representatives had to be set aside. The foundation was laid for that wonderful development of the realm of civil liberty—that field within which the individual is regarded as secured from governmental interference, the feature of our government which has called forth the highest praises of American statesmen and scholars—that realm of individual liberty guarded by the courts which permitted the freest and fullest develop-

[1] South Carolina, 1789, 1 Bay, 93; Maryland, 1802, 1 Harris and Johnson, 236; Tennessee, 1807, 1 Overton, 243; Ohio, 1829, 4 Ohio, 291, 17 Ohio, 125; for other cases in states, *cf. supra*, chap. 1.

ment of private rights the world has yet seen. This is the characteristic feature of our government which receives the unstinted praises of our great publicists, Lieber [1] and Burgess. Professor Burgess refers to this practice when he states that " while it must be confessed that we can learn much from the European constitutions in the organization of government and in the details of administration, yet for a clearly defined and well secured civil liberty,—one which can defy government, and still be subject to the state, one which can do far more for civilization upon many sides, and upon many of its finer sides, than the best ordered governments which the world has ever produced, — Europe must come to us and take lessons in the school of our experience, . . . let us never forget that constitutional civil liberty is the peculiar product of our political genius." [2]

---

[1] Lieber, *Civil Liberty and Self Government,* pp. 41, 167.

[2] Burgess, *Political Science and Constitutional Law,* i, p. 264.

CHAPTER V

PRINCIPLES OF THE JACKSONIAN DEMOCRACY

1. Democratic influence on the decisions of the Supreme Court

PRIOR to 1825, the friends of the doctrine of judicial supremacy had little occasion to be alarmed over the protests of those who denounced the practices of the courts. The resistance of the democratic party and the confirmed opposition of Jefferson did not hinder the federal courts from interfering freely with the legislative enactments of the states; and later when the policies of the time were tending in the direction of a stronger national government, this same party found the Supreme Court a powerful aid in the development of some of its leading projects.

But when the wave of enthusiasm which carried Jackson into office began to assert itself in the government it was to be expected that the Supreme Court would come in for its share of censure. Everything of an aristocratic nature was hateful to this new democracy. The life tenure ot the Supreme Court justices and the transcendent powers claimed for the judiciary were two features of the old order which the Jacksonian type of democrat heartily deplored. The rise of a regular party organization with radical views led to a renewal of the attacks upon the doctrine of judicial nullification.

On April 7th, 1826, Martin Van Buren, one of the leaders of the new party, expressed an opinion in the Senate which was intended to call attention to the dangers inherent in the

American doctrine. His remarks were prefaced by the admission that "there exists not upon this earth and there never did exist a judicial tribunal clothed with powers so various and so important as the Supreme Court."[1] Since the acts of Congress depend upon the court for their execution, and since the court can determine whether an act is in accord with the Constitution or not, the veto of the court, it is claimed, may absolutely suspend nine-tenths of the acts of the national legislature. Although the power has been rarely exercised its existence and an occasional interference are enough to serve as such a positive barrier as to be greatly deplored. Van Buren protested,

Not only are the acts of the national legislature subject to its review, but it stands as the umpire between the conflicting powers of the general and state governments. That wide field of debatable ground between those rival powers is claimed to be subject to the exclusive and absolute dominion of the Supreme Court. The discharge of this solemn duty has not been infrequent, and certainly not uninteresting. In virtue of this power, we have seen it holding for naught the statutes of powerful states, which had received the deliberate sanction, not only of their legislatures but of their judicatories. . . . You have seen such statutes abrogated by the decision of this court, and those confident in the wisdom and power of the state authorities plunged in irremediable ruin—decisions final in their effect and ruinous in their consequences. I speak of the power of the court, not of the correctness or incorrectness of its decisions. With that we have here nothing to do.[2]

After dealing with the fact that the highest authorities of almost every state in turn had been rebuked by the court in the exercise of this prerogative, Van Buren indicated the

---

[1] *Elliott's Debates*, iv, 485.　　　　[2] *Ibid.*, 485.

weakness of his objections by the admission that " the authority has been given to them, and this is not the place to mention its exercise." [1]   His remarks were closed with the reflection " that there is no known judicial power so transcendently omnipotent as that of the Supreme Court of the United States." [2]   It remained for President Jackson and Chief Justice Taney to indicate the method by which the principles announced by Marshall might be modified and the practice of judicial nullification restricted.

Second Conflict with Georgia.   The last great problem with which the Supreme Court had to deal while under the direction of Chief Justice Marshall was a conflict with the state of Georgia over the Indian question.   The issue arose through an attempt of the authorities of the state to secure control over the land of the Creeks.   The governor and legislature of Georgia openly defied the President of the United States and resisted the assertion of his authority under treaties with the Indians.   Congress was not inclined to stand by President Adams, and Georgia proceeded against the Indians according to her own discretion. [3]   After the contest had continued for more than two years, during which time a voluminous correspondence had merely tended to reveal the weakness of federal power and to arouse the wrath of the state authorities, the suggestion was made that the whole case be turned over to the Supreme Court of the United States.   The governor advised the state representatives in Congress that he could not acknowledge a power in the federal government to bring before its judicial tribunals for trial and judgment the governor, judges, or representatives of the state.   He was not wanting, the gov-

---

[1] *Elliott's Debates, op. cit.,* 487.   [2] *Ibid.,* 487.

[3] *House Executive Documents,* 19th Congress, second session. iv, no. 59; *Reports of House Committees,* iii, no. 98.

ernor claimed, in confidence in the Supreme Court of the United States, in all cases falling within its acknowledged jurisdiction. But according to his conception the Supreme Court was not made the arbiter in controversies involving rights of sovereignty between the states and the United States. The states could not therefore consent " to refer to the Supreme Court, as of right and obligation, questions of sovereignty between them and the United States, because that court, being of exclusive appointment by the government of the United States, will make the United States the judge of their own cause; this reason is equally applicable to a state tribunal." [1] The failure of Congress to support the President in his attempt to enforce the treaties and uphold national authority finally led to the acknowledgment of the contention of the state and brought an end to the Creek controversy.

Cherokee controversy. The success in the case of the Creeks led the authorities of Georgia to attempt to secure the lands of the Cherokees. This Indian tribe, with the tacit support of the United States government, drew up a constitution and took steps in the direction of setting up an independent government. This was directly in line with the past policy of the national government toward the Indians, treating them as independent communities within the states, to be dealt with by the national government and then only by treaty. Georgia retaliated by an act of assembly incorporating the land of the Cherokee nation into the territory of the state, and annulling all laws as well as the constitution of the newly formed nation. [2]

When the state authorities had shown every indication of incorporating the Indian lands regardless of federal treaties,

---

[1] Niles *Register*, xxxi, p. 20.   [2] *Ibid.*, xxxviii, pp. 328, 329.

Mr. Wirt of Maryland, who had been secured as counsel for the Indians, wrote to Governor Gilmer. He reminded the Governor of the difference of opinion regarding the rights of Georgia to deal with the Indians, and suggested that, " fortunately there exists a tribunal before which this difference may be quietly and peaceably settled," namely, the Supreme Court of the United States.[1] The governor in reply charged Mr. Wirt with having encouraged the spirit of resistance against the state and with having fostered the idea that the state had usurped authority. Through such men as Mr. Wirt, the Governor thought, the Cherokees were persuaded that the right of self-government could be secured for them by the power of the Supreme Court, in defiance of the legislation of the general and state governments.[2] "Your suggestion," the Governor continued, " is but an evidence of the state of that contest in which advocates of power are exerting themselves to increase the authority of the departments of the general government, whilst the friends of liberty and the rights of the people are in opposition, endeavoring to sustain the sovereignty of the states." [3]

The opportunity to bring the question at issue before the Supreme Court was soon presented when, in the execution of the statutes over the Cherokee territory, an Indian by the name of Corn Tassel was tried, convicted and sentenced to death. On an appeal to the Supreme Court a writ of error was granted with the purpose of bringing the case before the federal courts for reconsideration.

The Governor, having received the order from the court, submitted a message in which he referred to a communication, " purporting to be signed by the Chief Justice of the United States, and to be a citation of the state of Georgia

[1] Niles, *op. cit.*, xxxix, p. 69.

[2] *Ibid.*, p. 70.   [3] *Ibid.*, p. 71.

to appear before the Supreme Court, . . . to answer to that tribunal for having caused a person who had committed murder within the limits of the state, to be tried and convicted therefore," and he declared it to be his intention to resist the execution of the writ " with whatever force the laws have placed at my command." [1] The legislature immediately resolved, " that they view with feelings of deepest regret, the interference by the Chief Justice of the Supreme Court of the United States, in the administration of the criminal laws of the state, and that such an interference is a flagrant violation of her rights," and further that the governor and every other officer of the state are hereby requested to disregard any and every mandate that may be served upon him or them, purporting to proceed from the Chief Justice or any associate justice of the Supreme Court of the United States, for the purpose of arresting the execution of any criminal laws of the state.[2] The order of the Supreme Court was utterly ignored and Tassel was executed according to the verdict of the state tribunal.[3]

A later case was dismissed by the Supreme Court for want of jurisdiction, but with some caustic remarks from the court.[4] In delivering the opinion, Chief Justice Marshall reviewed briefly the history of the proceedings, and held that the numerous treaties made with the Indians by the United States recognized them " as a people capable of maintaining the relations of peace and war, of being responsible in their political character for any violation of their engagements, or for any aggression committed on the citizens of the United States by any individual of their community. Laws have been enacted in the spirit of these

---

[1] Niles, *op. cit.*, p. 338.

[2] *Ibid.*, p. 338.   [3] *Ibid.*, p. 353.

[4] Cherokee *vs.* The State of Georgia, 5 Peters, 1.

treaties. The acts of our government plainly recognize the
Cherokee nation as a state, and the courts are bound by
these acts." [1]   They had established a constitution and
form of government, the leading features of which were bor-
rowed from that of the United States.   Nevertheless
Georgia had assumed authority contrary to these laws and
treaties of the United States.   Corn Tassel, a Creek Indian
having been arrested in the Cherokee territory under process issued under the laws of Georgia, had been hanged in
defiance of a writ of error allowed by the Chief Justice of
the Supreme Court to the final sentence of the court of
Georgia.   If courts were permitted to indulge their sym-
pathies, Marshall thought, a case better calculated to expiate
them could scarcely be imagined.   The request of the
Indians was denied, however, because the court believed that
" the bill requires us to control the legislature of Georgia,
and to restrain the exertion of its physical course.   The
propriety of such an imposition by the court may well be
questioned.   It savors too much of the exercise of political
power to be within the province of the judicial department
. . .   If it be true that wrongs have been inflicted and that
still greater ones are to be apprehended, this is not the
tribunal which can redress the past or prevent the future." [2]

A new law of the state imposing more stringent regulations for the Cherokee territory was defied by several missionaries who were working among the Indians, with the
result that they were tried, convicted and sentenced to imprisonment. [3]   On application to the Supreme Court another writ was issued demanding that the authorities of the
state appear before the court.   Governor Lumpkin, instead

---

[1] Cherokee *vs*. The State of Georgia, 5 Peters, 15.

[2] 5 Peters, 19, 20.

[3] Niles, *op. cit.*, xl, pp. 244-248.

of obeying the writ, referred the whole matter to the legislature in a message which is very typical of the attitude assumed when the courts of the nation asserted jurisdiction over matters with which the state governments were inclined to deal and to admit of no interference. " My respect for the Supreme Court of the United States," said the governor, " as a fundamental department of the federal government, induces me to indulge the earnest hope, that no mandate will ever proceed from that court, attempting or intending to control one of the sovereign states of this union, in the free exercise of its constitutional, criminal or civil jurisdiction." [1] The object of the proceeding was considered to be nothing less than an attempt to call into question and to overthrow the essential jurisdiction of the state.

The Supreme Court not only assumed jurisdiction but decided the case against the state in no uncertain language. [2] The court, in the opinion submitted by Chief Justice Marshall, declared that the treaties and laws of the United States contemplated the Indian territory as completely separated from that of the state and provided that all intercourse with them should be carried on exclusively by the government of the Union.

The Cherokee nation, then, is a distinct community, occupying its own territory with boundaries accurately described, in which the laws of Georgia have no right to enter but with the assent of the Cherokees themselves, or in conformity with treaties, and with the acts of Congress. The whole intercourse between the United States and this nation is, by our Constitution and laws vested in the government of the United States. The act of the state of Georgia under which the

[1] Niles, *op. cit.*, p. 313.
[2] Worcester *vs.* The State of Georgia, 6 Peters, 515.

plaintiff in error was prosecuted is consequently void and the judgment a nullity.[1]

The mandate which was issued in accordance with this decision was totally disregarded. There were opinions in the press of the state strongly favoring the use of force and frequent references were made to the dangers of judicial despotism.[2] The case was supposed to demonstrate the absurdity of the doctrine that the federal courts were granted a supreme and absolute control over the states.

In the controversy with the Creeks the state authorities succeeded in gaining control of the lands because Congress failed to uphold President Adams in his attempt to enforce the treaties with the Indians. The Supreme Court was humiliated in the Cherokee difficulty because President Jackson supported the policy of the state government. In his first annual message, on December 8th, 1829, the President informed the country that

If the general government is not permitted to tolerate the erection of a confederate state within the territory of one of the members of this Union against her consent, much less could it allow a foreign and independent government to establish itself there.

Actuated by this view of the subject, I informed the Indians inhabiting parts of Georgia and Alabama that their attempt to establish an independent government would not be countenanced by the Executive of the United States, and advised them to emigrate beyond the Mississippi or submit to the laws of those states.[3]

As a result of the lack of unity of action among the

---

[1] 6 Peters, 560, 561.   [2] Niles, *op. cit.*, xlii, p. 78.
[3] Richardson, *Messages and Papers of the Presidents*, ii, pp. 457, 458.

departments of the federal government, Georgia felt at liberty to resist judicial mandates and enforce her own laws regardless of orders from the federal courts. The missionaries were finally pardoned by the governor, and the great question at issue was then settled by an act of Congress providing for the removal of all Indian tribes to the territory beyond the Mississippi River.[1] A few references to the controversy are to be found in the campaign literature of the time, when the failure of the President to secure the enforcement of federal judicial decrees was used as political capital against Jackson and his party.[2]

The successful resistance of Georgia in this dispute was a decided victory for the democrats, and in connection with the bank controversy where the authority of the court was successfully challenged from another quarter, may be looked upon as the beginning of a new era in the history of the court: an era when many questions heretofore determined by the court were voluntarily turned over to the political departments of the government; when the doctrine of implied powers, under which the authority of the federal government had been greatly enlarged, received a more restricted application; when the states were given a greater freedom from interference by the federal judiciary. It was the period which led to a reversal of the nationalistic policies of Hamilton and Marshall and a return to the principles of Jefferson and Jackson. The federalist party lost control of its only stronghold; the democratic party, for the first time, held full sway in all departments of the government. Four of the fundamental policies of the government pointed toward a strict construction of the Constitution. These were: the treatment of the Indians, the re-

---

[1] *United States Statutes at Large*, iv, 411, 412.
[2] *Works of Daniel Webster*, i, p. 269; Niles, *op. cit.*, xliii, 140.

fusal of the United States government to take part in internal improvements, the reduction of the tariff, and the attack upon the national bank.

The issue on the national bank raised a constitutional question of prime importance. The Supreme Court, in the case of McCulloch *vs.* Maryland [1] and later in the case of Osborne *vs.* the United States [2] had emphatically upheld the United States government in the establishment of a national bank. The great argument against the bank was on the ground of its unconstitutionality. This argument had been exhaustively treated by the court and strongly denied. The bank had continued to do business under a charter granted by Congress and was upheld in all its features by the Supreme Court of the United States.

National bank issue. Jackson and his party associates detested the bank. Its power, prestige, and it was charged, some of its money, had been used to perpetuate the federal administration of Adams. The corporation was attacked on all sides, but in no way so emphatically as on the issue of its unconstitutionality. In spite of a special message from the President against the bank, both houses of Congress voted to re-charter the corporation. [3] In the forceful veto with which Jackson returned the bill to Congress we have the President's opinion on judicial powers. [4]

It is maintained by the advocates of the bank that its constitutionality in all its features ought to be considered as settled by precedent and by the decisions of the Supreme Court. To this conclusion I cannot assent. . . . If the opinion of the Supreme Court covered the whole ground of this act, it

[1] 4 Wheaton, 316, 1819.   [2] 9 Wheaton, 738, 1824.

[3] *Senate Journal,* 22nd Congress, first session, pp. 451-453, July, 1832.

[4] *Ibid.,* pp. 433-446.

ought not to control the co-ordinate authorities of this government. The Congress, the executive and the court must each for itself be guided by its own opinion of the Constitution. Each public officer who takes an oath to support the Constitution swears that he will support it as he understands it, and not as it is understood by others. It is as much the duty of the House of Representatives, of the Senate, and of the President, to decide upon the constitutionality of any bill or resolution which may be presented to them for passage or approval, as it is of the Supreme Court when it may be brought before them for judicial decision. The opinion of the judges has no more authority over Congress than the opinion of Congress has over the judges; and, on that point, the President is independent of both. The authority of the Supreme Court must not, therefore, be permitted to control the Congress or the executive when acting in their legislative capacities, but to have only such influence as the force of their reasoning may deserve.[1]

The President continued to the effect that the issue of the kind or necessity of a banking institution was a question exclusively for legislative consideration. It was the province of the President and the legislature to determine whether a banking institution was necessary and to fix the powers and duties of such an institution and from their decision there was no appeal to the courts of justice.[2] In short, the President insisted that the legislative and executive departments had the ultimate authority to determine the constitutionality as well as the expediency of a national bank.

Change in the opinions of the court. Chief Justice Marshall lived to see two decided reversals of the principles upon which he had been building a unique constitutional structure. He had seen many of his efforts in enlarging the

[1] *Senate Journal, op. cit.,* pp. 438, 439. [2] *Ibid.,* p. 439.

field of authority of the central government and in humbling the states of the Union, sanctioned by the nation. He had taken advantage of the opportunity to lay the foundation for a strong central government out of the vague and indefinite provisions of a written instrument which left many questions open because of the fear that the possibilities of adoption might be jeopardized. His great appeal for broad and liberal principles of interpretation was made on the ground of expediency and necessity, and under the peculiar conditions of the time, his arguments were used with remarkable effect.

Many difficulties were arising, however, to embitter the closing years in the career of the Chief Justice. Georgia had successfully defied the authority of the court with the sympathetic support of the President and both houses of Congress. In addition, the President had turned the force of his logic against the doctrine that the Supreme Court was the final interpreter of the Constitution. A still greater difficulty arose when, after a careful consideration of two cases—Briscoe *vs.* Bank of Kentucky relative to a bank controversy and the City of New York *vs.* Miln, concerning the regulation of commerce, the Chief Justice was obliged to announce that

the practice of this court is, not (except in cases of absolute necessity) to deliver any judgment in cases where constitutional questions are involved, unless four judges concur in opinion, thus making the decision a majority of the whole court. In the present case four judges do not concur in opinion as to the constitutional question which had been argued. The court, therefore, directs these cases to be reargued at the next term under the expectation that a larger number of the judges may then be present.[1]

[1] 8 Peters, 121, 1834.

This was a confession on the part of Chief Justice Marshall that the federalist control of the judicial branch of the national government was losing ground. It was becoming clearer every day that a notable change in the political tenor of the government was affecting the trend of constitutional interpretation. The advocates of the extreme form of the American practice of judicial nullification of laws, which tended toward the enlargement of national control through the doctrine of implied powers and placed limitations on the realm of state action through an extensive application of a few general principles of the Constitution, had many reasons to be alarmed. Chief Justice Marshall lived long enough to get a slight glimpse into the period of strict construction. Fortunately, he was spared the chagrin which he would have been obliged to suffer as a result of criticisms and modifications of some of his greatest decisions.

2. *Opinions of Chief Justice Taney prior to 1856.*

With the appointment of Roger B. Taney to the Supreme Court, the dominant influence of Marshall and his old-time associates ceased. Justice Taney had served as Attorney-General under President Jackson at the time of the notable fight against the national bank, and was known to be in sympathy with the main policies of the democratic party. His appointment was purposely planned to place at the head of the court a justice who stood for a strict construction of the Constitution, a greater respect for the rights of the states and a reduction of judicial interference in the public affairs of the nation. Although Chief Justice Taney did not control the policy of the court as completely as Marshall had directed its course in the first period of our constitutional history, nevertheless his opinions indicate clearly the tendencies of the time.

The earlier opinions of the Chief Justice were characterized by a strict adherence to the language of the Constitution, the doctrine of implied powers was narrowly interpreted, and the principles of convenience and expediency were used to restrict the rapidly developing powers of the central government rather than to enlarge them. Taney was especially anxious to allow the fullest and freest exercise of authority by the states which a strict interpretation of the Constitution would permit. The result of such a policy was not likely to involve the federal courts in contests over the assertion of authority either with the states or the departments of the federal government. For a period of twenty years the main point to be considered is the method by which conflicts were avoided and judicial powers narrowly restricted in the opinions of a court controlled by men under the influence of democratic doctrines.

Charles River Bridge case. The first important case in which the principles of the Chief Justice were definitely applied was the contest between the Charles River Bridge and the Warren Bridge,[1] in which an old corporation attempted to restrain a newly organized company from building a bridge across the Charles River, claiming that its charter from the legislature gave an exclusive franchise and therefore the new law impaired the obligation of contract. On the principle that the charters to public corporations must be construed strictly, the Chief Justice arrived at the conclusion that the pretensions of the older corporation were unwarranted. It seems the state had not expressly given an exclusive contract, nor could the words of the charter be construed to furnish such a grant without a manifest stretch of interpretation. The customary method of Marshall, of basing his opinion, at least partially, upon the political doctrine of expediency, was here used against the right of judicial interference. Chief Justice Taney argued

[1] 11 Peters, 420, 1837.

It would present a singular spectacle if, while the courts in England are restraining, within the strictest limits, the spirit of monopoly, and exclusive privileges in nature of monopolies, and confining corporations to the privileges plainly given to them in their charter, the courts of this country should be found enlarging these privileges by implication, and construing a statute more unfavorably to the public and to the rights of the community than would be done in a like case in an English court of justice.[1] . . .

If this court should establish the principles now contended for, what is to become of the numerous railroads established on the same line of travel with turnpike companies, and which have rendered the franchises of the turnpike corporations of no value? Let it once be understood that such charters carry with them these implied contracts. . . . We shall be thrown back to the improvements of the last century, and obliged to stand still until the claims of the old turnpike corporations shall be satisfied and they shall consent to permit these states to avail themselves of the lights of modern science and to partake of the benefits of those improvements which are now adding to the wealth and prosperity, and the convenience and comfort, of every part of the civilized world.[2]

The danger of placing restrictions around state control of private corporations was plainly foreseen in the remark that " the continued existence of a government would be of no great value, if by implications and presumptions, it was disarmed of the powers necessary to accomplish the ends of its creation; and the functions it was designed to perform, transferred to the hands of privileged corporations." [3]

It was asserted that ambiguity in the terms of the contract must operate against the corporation, and in favor of the public, and nothing could be claimed that was not clearly

---

[1] 11 Peters, 545.   [2] *Ibid.*, 552, 553.
[3] *Ibid.*, 547.

given by the act of incorporation. A doctrine of interpretation was then announced which was very different from that which the court had been accustomed to follow.

The object and end of all government is to promote the happiness and prosperity of the community by which it is established; and it can never be assumed that the government intended to diminish its power of accomplishing the end for which it was created. . . . A state ought never to presume to surrender this power, because, like the taxing power, the whole community have an interest in preserving it undiminished.[1] . . . No one will question that the interest of the great body of the people of the state would, in this instance, be affected by the surrender of this great line of travel to a single corporation, with the right to exact toll and exclude competition for seventy years. While the rights of private property are sacredly guarded, we must not forget that the community also have rights, and that the happiness and wellbeing of every citizen depends on their faithful preservation.[2]

The rights of private property, so jealously guarded in the provisions of the Constitution and so strongly upheld in many of the decisions of the Supreme Court, had to give way, on the basis of a strict interpretation of the charter, to what was regarded as the manifestly greater principle of public necessity.

Justice Story dissented from the opinion of the court in vigorous language, following the reasoning of a day of judicial interpretation whose sun had set a few years before. In a letter to Justice McClean, Story lamented that " there will not, I fear, ever in our day be any case in which a law of a state or act of Congress will be declared unconstitutional; for the old constitutional doctrines are

---

[1] 11 Peters, 547.   [2] *Ibid.*, 548.

fast fading away, and a change has come over the public mind from which I augur little good." [1] A few years later Justice Story felt obliged to resign because he was, as he said, in a dead minority and was forced regularly to dissent from the opinions of the court or acquiesce in principles with which he was not at all in sympathy. In a letter stating his reasons for resigning, he said,.

I have long been convinced that the doctrines and opinions of the " old court " were daily losing ground, and especially those on great constitutional questions. New men and new opinions have succeeded. The doctrines of the Constitution, so vital to the country which in former times received the support of the whole court, no longer maintained their ascendency. I am the last member now living of the old court, and I cannot consent to remain where I can no longer hope to see these doctrines recognized and enforced. [2]

Restrictions on the realm of judicial authority. The exception to the broad doctrine of judicial control of all governmental functions admitted by Chief Justice Marshall in the Marbury case, [3] was seized upon to narrow the authority of the courts. The realm within which the President and the legislature were to have discretionary powers was widened in an attempt to confine the authority of the courts to the determination of judicial questions. Instead of drawing cases into the field of judicial cognizance, the proposition was announced in a dissenting opinion that " the powers given to the courts of the United States by the Constitution are judicial powers, and extend to those subjects, only,

---

[1] *Life and Letters of Joseph Story*, edited by W. W. Story, ii, p. 272; also New York Review, April, 1838, vol. ii, p. 372.

[2] *Letters of Story, op. cit.*, pp. 527, 528.

[3] Marbury *vs.* Madison, 1 Cranch, 165; *cf. supra*, p. 69.

which are judicial in character and not to those that are political." [1] Chief Justice Taney went so far as to claim that the rights of sovereignty and jurisdiction between states were not subjects of judicial cognizance. [2] A question relative to the disposition of Indian lands, somewhat similar to the earlier cases of this nature, which had caused so much difficulty for the courts, was readily disposed of by the admission that " it is a question for the law-making and political departments of the government, and not for the judicial. It is our duty to expound and execute the law as we find it." [3]

No great advance was required to reach the opinion of Calhoun regarding the power of the Supreme Court. As between the parties to a suit he thought the decision of this tribunal must be final. But its judgments could not be binding between the United States and the individual states, " as neither can make the other defendant in any controversy between them." [4]

In the great majority of cases throughout this period the court was not disposed to interfere with the other departments of the government. Frequently cases which had been decided heretofore by the Supreme Court were disposed of by reminding the parties concerned that these questions must be determined by the political departments of the government. A controversy growing out of Dorr's rebellion in Rhode Island led to a noteworthy opinion by the Chief Justice. [5] Much of the argument on the part of the plaintiff turned upon political rights and political questions on which the court had been urged to express an opinion.

[1] State of Rhode Island vs. State of Massachusetts, 12 Peters, 752.
[2] 12 Peters, 753.   [3] United States vs. Rogers, 4 Howard, 572.
[4] Works of Calhoun, i, pp. 264, 265.
[5] Luther vs. Borden, 7 Howard, 1.

We decline doing so.   The high power has been conferred on this court of passing judgment upon the acts of state sovereignties, and of the legislative and executive branches of the federal government, and of determining whether they are beyond the limits of power marked out for them respectively by the Constitution of the United States.   This tribunal, therefore, should be the last to overstep the boundaries which limits its own jurisdiction. And while it should always be ready to meet any question confided to it by the Constitution, it is equally its duty not to pass beyond its appropriate sphere of action, and to take care not to involve itself in discussions which properly belong to other forums.[1]

The determination of the question here brought before the court, it was held, was clearly a political issue and belonged to the political departments of the government—Congress and the President. The logical conclusion was accepted that when a state changed its form of government and the political authorities of the nation recognized the change, the courts were bound to accept such recognition in future decisions.

When the majority of the court was disposed to condemn a bridge across the Ohio River as a nuisance which the laws of the United States did not permit, the Chief Justice delivered a strong dissenting opinion.[2]   Assuming, he argues, that the bridge does obstruct a public, navigable river, such as the Ohio, which at common law would be a nuisance, is this court authorized to declare it such and abate it?[3]   It is admitted that Congress may prohibit obstructions in or upon the river but it has not done so.   But if Congress has not thought proper or does not think it

[1] 7 Howard, 47.

[2] Pennsylvania *vs.* Wheeling Bridge Company, 13 Howard, 518.

[3] 13 Howard, 579.

proper, to exercise this power, and public mischief has arisen, or may arise from it, it does not follow that the judicial power of the United States may step in and supply what the legislative authority has omitted to perform.[1] The Chief Justice was arguing against the tendency in courts to legislate by means of judicial decisions.

Maintenance of rights of the states. An equally significant feature of the opinions handed down by Chief Justice Taney was his insistence upon the maintenance of the reserved rights of the states. His main contention was that the states could not be restrained within narrower limits than those fixed by the Constitution of the United States, and that within these limits they were the sole judges of what was best for their own interests.

In Prigg *vs.* the Commonwealth of Pennsylvania where the majority opinion of the court, delivered by Story, a few years before his resignation, maintained that the power of legislation on the subject of fugitives from labor was exclusively in Congress, Chief Justice Taney agreed in the judgment but denounced a part of the opinion of Story as an unjustifiable interference with state legislation.[2] In the absence of any express prohibition, he could perceive no reason for establishing one by implication. But it was in the License cases [3] that the Chief Justice took even a firmer stand in preserving the integrity of state authority. The states had attempted to regulate the liquor traffic and had come into conflict with the principles laid down by the Supreme Court in the case of Brown *vs.* Maryland. At the very opening of his opinion Taney discarded the principle upheld in some of the earlier cases, in the words,

It is equally clear that the power of Congress over this sub

[1] 13 Howard, 581, 582.   [2] 16 Peters, 626-633.
[3] 5 Howard, 504.

ject does not extend further than the regulation of commerce
with foreign nations and among the several states; and that
beyond these limits the states never have surrendered their
power over trade and commerce, and may still exercise it free
from any controlling power on the part of the central government. Every state, therefore, may regulate its own internal
traffic according to its own judgment and upon its own views
of the interest and well-being of its citizens.[1]

Men of the time argued that the regulation of commerce
was given exclusively to the general government, and that
even if Congress did not regulate, the states could not; if
Congress enacted legislation all state laws to the contrary
had to give way, but the real issue was whether the states
could regulate at all. The Supreme Court had been inclined
toward the view of an exclusive grant to Congress. The
Chief Justice answered this contention by stating that " the
controlling and supreme power over commerce with foreign
nations and the several states is undoubtedly conferred upon
Congress. Yet, in my judgment, the states may nevertheless, for the safety or convenience of trade, or for the protection of the health of its citizens, make regulations of
commerce for its own ports and harbors, and for its own
territory; and such regulations are valid unless they come
into conflict with a law of Congress." [2] This judgment of
Chief Justice Taney was upheld by the later developments
in decisions on commercial questions.[3]

The instances noted represent but a few of the cases in
which the doctrines of Marshall were modified on the
ground that they were not warranted by the Constitution.

---

[1] 5 Howard, 574.   [2] *Ibid.*, 579.

[3] See Leisy *vs.* Harden, 135 *United States Reports*, 100 and *In re*
Rahrer, 140 *United States Reports*, 545.

3. The development of a judicial tradition.

It must not be supposed that the doctrines of the court under the direction of Chief Justice Taney tended toward a denial of the right of judicial nullification. The Chief Justice took occasion to reaffirm this right,[1] although it was seldom exercised. In spite of the restrictive features of Taney's opinions, the main principles of judicial interpretation which had been formulated by Marshall were gradually developing into a judicial tradition which grew stronger even in the period of democratic ascendency.

Those who ordinarily were inclined toward the doctrine of a strict interpretation of the Constitution began to accept the idea that the Supreme Court was the proper body to determine the ultimate validity of laws. Madison's last letter relative to judicial powers shows the change in attitude which may be frequently noticed throughout the period from 1820 to 1850. Having once firmly upheld the view that the legislature must be granted an equal right with the courts in determining the constitutionality of laws, Madison now reiterated this doctrine.[2] He merely repeated the old idea of a coördination of powers among the three departments, and then claimed that in case of irreconcilable interpretations the supremacy of one department or another must depend on the nature of the issue. But since the judicial department attracts the greatest public confidence and has the advantage of discussion which the Executive does not possess and which the composite nature of the legislative department would not permit, this department, it was submitted, will " most engage the respect and reliance of the public as the surest expositor of the Constitution, as well in questions within its cognizance concerning the boundaries

---

[1] Notably Luther vs. Borden, 7 Howard, 47; cf. supra, p. 139.

[2] Works of Madison, iv, p. 349, 1834.

between the several departments of the government as in those between the Union and its members." [1]

The development of the traditional view is best expressed in the speeches of Daniel Webster. As a disciple of Hamilton and an advocate of some of the most important doctrines formulated in the judicial opinions of Marshall, Webster was well qualified to impress upon the public in address and legal argument, the importance of such a tribunal as the Supreme Court. When the possibility of democratic control of the government was assured, and the powers of the court were assailed, Webster warned the people that if men were placed in the supreme tribunal of the country who entertained opinions hostile to the just powers of the Constitution, the nation would be visited by an evil defying all remedies. [2] He constantly feared the change in the membership of the judiciary. " No conviction is deeper in my mind," Webster affirmed, " than that the maintenance of the judicial power is essential and indispensable to the very being of this government. The Constitution without it would be no constitution; the government, no government." [3] The judiciary was thought to be the protecting power of the whole government. Webster believed no higher tribunal existed than the Supreme Court of the United States, because it was the expounder of fundamental principles of government, the appointed umpire on questions of the profoundest interest between conflicting sovereignties. [4] The judicial department, having the full right to declare laws unconstitutional, was regarded by him as the very foundation of the American system, and he was persuaded that the Union could not exist without a

---

[1] *Works of Madison,* iv, p. 350.

[2] *Works of Daniel Webster,* i, p. 212.

[3] *Ibid.,* iii, p. 176.   [4] *Ibid.,* ii, pp. 402, 403.

supreme court exercising paramount authority over all national questions.

This view of the great importance and transcendent authority of the judicial department finally impressed itself upon a court composed even of strict constructionists, to such an extent that contrary to many of their former opinions, an attempt was made to settle through judicial authority a political question which had baffled a succession of Presidents and had engaged the attention of every Congress for more than twenty years.

CHAPTER VI

JUDICIAL POWERS FROM 1856 TO 1870

1. Courts become involved in the slavery controversy

Dred Scott decision. As early as 1848, it was suggested in Congress that the issues involved in the slavery controversy be turned over to the Supreme Court for final determination. It seemed quite clear, however, that the court, in accordance with its policy of avoiding political issues, would not render a judgment even if it were possible to present the questions in the form of a case. It was thought that a decision of the Supreme Court would not satisfy both parties, and that its decisions would be disregarded as had been the case in the bank controversy. Certain members of Congress then intimated that although the people had respect for the Supreme Court, they were not willing to leave the decision to a court so large a portion of which were opposed to slavery.[1] Nevertheless from 1848 to 1856 the idea of settling the slavery issue by judicial determination was evident in several cases which were brought before the state courts.[2]

It would be useless to attempt to add anything here to the discussion as to the way in which the Dred Scott case arose. Neither will an effort be made to give a complete analysis of the decision itself, with concurring and dissenting opinions, nor will it be possible to include any ex-

[1] *Debates of Congress* (abridgment), vol. xvi, pp. 225-229.
[2] *Ibid.,* p. 226.

tended account of the voluminous discussions which grew out of the decision. The whole case will be treated, primarily, so as to indicate its relation to the judicial controversies which had preceded it and those which were soon to follow. The case was brought to the Supreme Court from the circuit court for the district of Missouri, was twice argued, and a decision was finally reached in which all except two justices concurred.[1]   A judgment was rendered to the effect that the circuit court did not have jurisdiction because Dred Scott was not a citizen of Missouri and could not therefore according to the Constitution of the United States maintain an action in the federal courts.[2]   This was the real issue presented on the record, and the courts might have closed the case with this judgment. But no doubt some of the members thought that a determination of the difficult question of the rights of slavery in the territories could be brought within the case, and thus be finally settled. The opinion of the court given by the Chief Justice therefore took up this question, and held that the power of Congress over the territories acquired since the adoption of the Constitution was limited by all the provisions in favor of private rights; that the Missouri compromise was necessarily unconstitutional; and that Congress could not prohibit slavery within the territories.[3]

In his opinion the Chief Justice announced, " it is not the province of the court to decide upon the justice or injustice, the policy or impolicy of these laws. The decision of that question belonged to the political or law-making power." The duty of the court was held to be the inter-

---

[1] Dred Scott *vs.* Sanford, 19 Howard, 393; for a brief history of the case see Burgess, *The Middle Period,* chapter xxi, " The Dred Scott Case."

[2] 19 Howard, pp. 426, 427.   [3] *Ibid.,* pp. 447-454.

pretation of the Constitution.[1] Justice Wayne said that the court had neither sought nor made the case, but that the justices had only discharged their duty as provided in the Constitution. He thought it a matter for congratulation that " the opinion of the court meets fully and decides every point which was made in the argument of the case by the counsel on either side of it." [2] Just a few days before this opinion was read, President Buchanan said that the question which had so agitated the nation during the previous campaign was a matter of little practical importance. " Besides," he suggested, " it is a judicial question, which legitimately belongs to the Supreme Court of the United States, before whom it is now pending, and will, it is understood, be speedily and finally settled. To their decision, in common with all good citizens, I shall cheerfully submit, whatever this may be." [3]

But two members of the court were not so fully convinced that the Constitution placed this duty upon the court, nor did they believe that many of the points ostensibly determined in the majority opinion ought to have the force of law. Several extracts from the opinion of Justice Curtis, in which he attempts to overthrow every argument of the Chief Justice, will serve to show the attitude of a judicial mind toward the doctrines announced by the court. After having given an answer to the first part of the decision, Justice Curtis remarked:

On so grave a subject as this, I feel obliged to say that, in my opinion, such an exertion of judicial power transcends the limits of authority of the court, as described by its repeated decisions, and, as I understand, acknowledged in this

[1] 19 Howard, 405.   [2] *Ibid.*, 454.

[3] Richardson, *op. cit.*, v, 43.

opinion of the majority of the court. . . . I do not consider it to be within the scope of the judicial power of the majority of the court to pass upon any question respecting the plaintiff's citizenship in Missouri, save that raised by the plea to the jurisdiction; and I do not hold any opinion of this court, or any court, binding when expressed on a question not legitimately before it. The judgment of this court is, that the case is to be dismissed for want of jurisdiction, because the plaintiff was not a citizen of Missouri, as he alleged in his declaration. Into that judgment, according to the settled course of this court, nothing appearing after a plea to the merits can enter. A great question of constitutional law, deeply affecting the peace and welfare of the country, is not, in my opinion, a fit subject to be thus reached.[1]

And in concluding his answer to the second part of the decision he observed:

To allow this to be done with the Constitution, upon reasons purely political, renders its judicial interpretation impossible, because judicial tribunals, as such, cannot decide upon political considerations. Political reasons have not the requisite certainty to afford rules of judicial interpretation. They are different in different men. They are different in the same men at different times. And when a strict interpretation of the Constitution, according to the fixed rules which govern the interpretation of laws, is abandoned, and the theoretical opinions of individuals are allowed to control its meaning, we have no longer a Constitution; we are under the government of individual men, who for the time being have the power to declare what the Constitution is, according to their own views of what it ought to mean.[2]

Such a practice was plainly denounced as an attempt to foist

[1] 19 Howard, 589, 590.   [2] Ibid., 620, 621.

the individual opinions of the members of the Supreme Court upon the country, under the cloak of constitutional interpretation.

As soon as the decision was announced it was seized upon by both of the leading parties to be used for political purposes. The opinion of the Chief Justice was circulated by the democrats, the dissenting opinion of Justice Curtis, by the republicans.[1] On the one side it was maintained that, "whoever resists the final decisions of the highest judicial tribunal aims a deadly blow to our whole republican system of government."[2] On the other hand the opinion of Chief Justice Taney was denounced as deserving of no more respect than a pro-slavery stump speech delivered during the recent presidential campaign.[3] The contest was soon thrust into the political arena by the series of debates between Douglas and Lincoln in which the Dred Scott decision was one of the most important issues.

Views of Lincoln. In a speech at Springfield, Illinois, after having been named as the republican candidate for United States Senator, Lincoln made his first public attack upon the Supreme Court decision. He gave a history of what he regarded as the "complete legal machinery," that is, a combination between Senator Douglas, the President of the United States and the members of the Supreme Court, by which slavery was to be forever fastened upon the country. He impressed the idea upon the assembly by the illustration of framed timbers, the parts of which are made at different times and places by different workmen, but which when brought together fit exactly and form so com-

---

[1] Rhodes, *History of the United States*, ii, p. 264.

[2] Douglas to the grand jury at Springfield, Ill., published in the *New York Times*, June 23, 1857.

[3] Pike, *First Blows of the Civil War*, pp. 368, 370.

plete a structure in every part as to indicate that there must
have been a common plan.[1] Only one more decision,
Lincoln said, was necessary to force slavery upon the states.
That decision was sure to come unless the people met and
overthrew the power of the dynasty which had perpetrated
upon the country the first infamous decision.[2]

When taken to task by Judge Douglas for his resistance
to a decision of the Supreme Court, Lincoln replied that he
was not resisting the decision, or attempting to interfere
with property by taking Dred Scott from his master. "All
that I am doing," Lincoln said," is refusing to obey it as a
political rule. If I were in Congress and a vote should
come up on a question whether slavery should be prohibited
in a new territory, in spite of the Dred Scott decision I
would vote that it should . . . Somebody has to reverse
that decision, since it is made, and we mean to reverse it,
and we mean to do it peaceably."[3] Lincoln condemned
Judge Douglas because he insisted that this extraordinary
decision was to be accepted by Congress and obeyed by
everybody. The instance of the national bank was cited
wherein a decision of the Supreme Court was overruled by
the other departments of the government.[4]

As the debate progressed, Lincoln found it necessary to
take even stronger ground. On July 17th, he read from
the letter of Jefferson in which the idea was denounced that
the judges must be regarded as the final arbiters on all constitutional questions, and that the judges were to be held
in higher esteem than other men; and in which the assertion
was made that " the Constitution has erected no such single
tribunal, knowing that, to whatever hands confided, with
the corruptions of time and party, its members would be-

---

[1] *Lincoln and Douglas Debates*, pp. 1-5.   [2] *Ibid.*, p. 6.
[3] *Ibid.*, pp. 29, 30.   [4] *Ibid.*, pp. 30, 31.

come despots." [1]   Lincoln then remarked, " thus we see the power claimed for the Supreme Court by Judge Douglas, Mr. Jefferson holds, would reduce us to the despotism of an oligarchy.   Now, I have said no more than this, in fact, never quite so much as this; at least I am sustained by Mr. Jefferson." [2]   The instances wherein Supreme Court decisions had been disregarded and overturned were frequently cited with approval.

When attacked as to the way he proposed to resist the court's decision Lincoln replied,

We oppose the Dred Scott decision in a certain way, upon which I ought perhaps to address you a few words.   We do not propose that when Dred Scott has been decided to be a slave by the court, we, as a mob, will decide him to be free . . . but we nevertheless do oppose that decision as a political rule which shall be binding on the voter to vote for nobody who thinks it wrong, which shall be binding on the members of Congress or the President to favor no measure that does not actually concur with the principles of that decision. . . . We propose so resisting it as to have it reversed if we can, and a new judicial rule established upon this subject.[3]

Lincoln charged Douglas with favoring Supreme Court decisions when he liked them and opposing them when he did not like them,[4] and called his attention to the fact that the Cincinnati platform which the Judge was advocating unqualifiedly, disregarded a " time-honored decision of the Supreme Court, in denying the power of Congress to establish a national bank." [5]   In the opinion of Lincoln, the Dred Scott decision would never have been made had not

---

[1] *Works of Jefferson*, vol. xii, p. 163; *cf. supra*, p. 67.
[2] *Debates*, pp. 92, 93.   [3] *Ibid.*, p. 299.
[4] *Ibid.*, p. 94.   [5] *Ibid.*, p. 280.

the party that was responsible for it been previously sustained at the polls.[1]

The most direct attack upon the decision by Lincoln was embodied in a speech at Edwardsville, on September 13th, in which he referred to it as follows:

My friends, I have endeavored to show you the logical consequences of the Dred Scott decision, which holds that the people of a territory cannot prevent the establishment of slavery in their midst. I have stated, which cannot be gainsaid, that the grounds upon which this decision is made are equally applicable to the free states as to the free territories, and that the peculiar reasons put forth by Judge Douglas for endorsing this decision, commit him, in advance, to the next decision and to all other decisions coming from the same source. . . . What constitutes the bulwark of our own liberty and independence? . . . Our reliance is in the love of liberty which God has planted in us. Our defence is in the spirit which prized liberty as the heritage of all men, in all lands everywhere. Destroy this spirit and you have planted the seeds of despotism at your own doors. Familiarize yourselves with the chains of bondage and you prepare your own limbs to wear them. Accustomed to trample on the rights of others, you have lost the genius of your own independence and become the fit subjects of the first cunning tyrant who rises among you. And let me tell you, that all these things are prepared for you by the teachings of history, if the elections shall promise that the next Dred Scott decision and all future decisions will be quietly acquiesced in by the people.[2]

In a few of his later addresses Lincoln referred with ridicule to the " Dred Scott Supreme Court." [3] The fol-

[1] *Debates*, p. 279.
[2] Nicolay and Hay, *Works of Abraham Lincoln*, xi, pp. 109-111.
[3] *Debates*, p. 380.

lowing year the republican party resolved in its platform " that the new dogma that the Constitution, of its own force, carries slavery into any or all territories of the United States, is a dangerous political heresy, at variance with the explicit provisions of that instrument itself, with contemporaneous exposition, and with legislative and judicial precedent; is revolutionary in its tendency, and subversive of the peace and harmony of the country," [1] and rewarded one of the bitterest opponents of that dogma with the nomination to the greatest office in the country.

Views of Douglas. From the beginning Judge Douglas took issue with Lincoln relative to this decision, and made it one of the central points for criticism of Lincoln as well as of his party. A few days after Lincoln's first speech Douglas charged his opponent with instituting " a crusade against the Supreme Court of the United States," and then indicated his stand in regard to the decision: [2]

As a lawyer I feel at liberty to appear before the court and controvert any principle of law while the question is pending before the tribunal; but when the decision is made, my private opinion, your opinion, all other opinions, must yield to the majesty of that authoritative adjudication. . . . I have no idea of appealing from the decision of the Supreme Court upon a constitutional question to the decisions of a tumultuous town meeting. . . . I respect the decisions of that august tribunal; I shall always bow in deference to them.[3]

Unless we respect the final decisions of the highest judicial tribunal in our country, Judge Douglas continued, we are driven to anarchy, to violence, to mob law, and there is no security left to property or civil rights. Mr. Lincoln

[1] Stanwood, *History of the Presidency,* pp. 292, 293.
[2] *Debates,* pp. 15, 16.   [3] *Ibid.,* p. 16.

says he will reverse the decision, but how will he proceed? The Constitution makes the decision of the court final in regard to the validity of an act of Congress. But he is going to reverse that decision by passing another act of Congress,[1] or he is going to appeal to the people to elect a President who will disregard the decision.[2]

What good can it do, asked Douglas, to wage war upon the court, arraying it against Congress, and Congress against the court? Whenever partisan politics shall be carried on to the bench or the judges shall be arraigned upon the stump; whenever the independence and integrity of the judiciary shall be tampered with, there will be no security for your rights and your liberties. As a good citizen, Douglas asserted that he was bound to sustain the constituted authorities, and to resist, discourage and beat down all attempts at exciting mobs, or violence, or any other revolutionary proceedings against the Constitution.[3]

These remarks were followed a few days later by a bit of sarcasm directed at Lincoln's charges:

I have no comment to make on that part of Mr. Lincoln's speech in which he represents me as forming a conspiracy with the Supreme Court, and with the late President of the United States and the present chief magistrate, having for my object the passage of the Kansas-Nebraska bill, the Dred Scott decision, and the extension of slavery,—a scheme of political tricksters, composed of Chief Justice Taney and his eight associates, two Presidents of the United States and one Senator of Illinois. . . . All I have to say is that I do not think so badly of the President of the United States, and the Supreme Court of the United States, the highest judicial tribunal on earth, as to believe that they were capable in their action

---

[1] *Debates,* p. 49.   [2] *Ibid.,* p. 72.
[3] *Ibid.,* pp. 50, 51.

and decision of entering into political intrigues for partisan purposes.[1]

Douglas recurred on several occasions to the enormity of an insignificant individual like Lincoln, charging a conspiracy upon a large number of members of Congress, the Supreme Court, and two Presidents, to nationalize slavery.[2] He thought it unnecessary to go into an argument to prove whether or not Chief Justice Taney understood the law better than Abraham Lincoln.[3]   Douglas observed that he had never before heard of an appeal being taken to Congress to reverse a decision of the Supreme Court; but that appeals were usually taken from Congress to the Supreme Court.[4]

The Democratic convention which met at Charleston in April, 1860, adopted a series of resolutions including one to the effect that the democratic party would abide by the decisions of the Supreme Court on questions of constitutional law.[5]   The delegates who re-assembled at Baltimore, after the failure to come to an agreement at Charleston, passed a resolution almost unanimously upholding the decision relative to slavery in the territories as finally determined by the Supreme Court of the United States, and urging that this decision " be respected by all good citizens, and enforced with promptness and fidelity by every branch of the general government."[6]   The northern democrats chose as their standard-bearer Judge Douglas, who had so faithfully championed the cause of the supremacy of judicial decisions.

Resolutions from the states.   The sentiment in the northern states on the Dred Scott decision was shown in the resolutions adopted by several state assemblies.   Resolutions

[1] *Debates*, p. 66.

[3] *Ibid.*, p. 176.

[5] Stanwood, *op. cit.*, p. 283.

[2] *Ibid.*, p. 141.

[4] *Ibid.*, p. 72.

[6] Stanwood, p. 286.

from the state of Maine condemned the decision as follows:

The extra judicial opinion of the Supreme Court of the United States in the case of Dred Scott is not binding in law or conscience upon the government or citizens of the United States. . . . The Supreme Court of the United States should, by peaceful and constitutional measures, be so reconstituted as to relieve it from the domination of a sectional faction, and make it a tribunal whose decision shall be in harmony with the Constitution of the United States and the spirit of our institutions.[1]

Massachusetts resolved that,

While the people of Massachusetts recognize the rightful judicial authority of the Supreme Court of the United States in the determination of all questions properly coming before it, they will never consent that their rights shall be impaired, or their liberties invaded, by reason of any usurpations of political power by said tribunal.[2]

The general assembly of Connecticut declared that the majority of the judges of the Supreme Court, in the recent case of Dred Scott, " have departed from the usages which have heretofore governed our courts; have volunteered opinions which are not law; have given occasion for the belief that they promulgated such opinions for partisan purposes, and thereby have lowered the dignity of said court, and diminished the respect heretofore awarded to its decisions."[3]

Opinions in Congress. The democratic members of Congress rejoiced in the decision and insisted that the court's opinion as well as its judgment must be enforced and

[1] *Senate Miscellaneous Documents,* 35th Congress, first session, no. 14.

[2] *Senate Documents, op. cit.,* no. 231.   [3] *Ibid.,* no. 188.

obeyed. Expressions of opinion from democratic members, although occasionally quite extreme, added little to the masterly discussions of Judge Douglas. In the main the arguments in opposition followed the lines indicated by Lincoln.

The most prominent republican before the nomination to the presidency of Abraham Lincoln was Seward. His speeches in Congress and his public addresses were followed with keen interest. His thought regarding the Dred Scott decision was that " in this ill-omened act, the Supreme Court forgot its own dignity which had always before been maintained with just judicial jealousy . . . and they and the President alike forgot that judicial usurpation is more odious and intolerable than any other among the manifold practices of tyranny." [1] After denying that the court had jurisdiction in the case, Seward said, " they proceeded with amusing solemnity to pronounce the opinion, that if they had had such jurisdiction, still the unfortunate negro would have had to remain in bondage, unrelieved because the Missouri prohibition violates rights of general property involved in slavery, paramount to the authority of Congress." [2] And in suggesting a way out of the condition created by this unprecedented decision, he maintained that the Supreme Court could reverse its " spurious judgment " more easily than the people could be reconciled to its usurpation. [3]

The most extreme view was presented by Congressman Ashley in a paper on the " Success of the Calhoun Revolution," submitted on May 29th, 1860. Mr. Ashley brought the charge that from the beginning of Tyler's administration, the opinions of men on the slavery question were made the test for promotion to positions in the Supreme

[1] *Seward's Works,* iv, p. 586.
[2] *Ibid.,* p. 587.   [3] *Ibid.,* p. 595.

Court. He claimed that no man who entertained views hostile to the interests and political opinions of the Calhoun party could secure a place on the Supreme Bench.[1] Mr. Ashley further asserted that able and worthy men were not considered by the judiciary committee. To the political opinions of a court thus constituted, he found, the people of the United States were called upon to bow in submission, and were denounced as traitors to the Constitution and the Union unless they yielded their political views and embraced those of a majority of this " packed and irresponsible tribunal." [2] The gist of the whole controversy was summed up by a member of Congress in the statement that the democratic party resolved to abide by the decisions of the Supreme Court of the United States over the institution of slavery within the territories, while, on the other hand, the republican party intended in the coming election to refer this question to the American people, believing that they were the arbiters of all political questions, and denying that the Supreme Court could decide the great political questions of the day.[3]

Defiance from Wisconsin.   Just prior to the outbreak of the war, Wisconsin defied the authority of the Supreme Court and advocated an extreme states-rights doctrine. The supreme court of Wisconsin had declared the fugitive slave law unconstitutional,[4] and the enforcement of the law by federal authority was stoutly resisted by state officers. On a writ of *habeas corpus* issued by the state court, Booth, who had taken part in the rescue of a slave was released, and apparently the federal authorities were worsted. The decision of the supreme court of Wisconsin was finally re-

---

[1] *Congressional Globe*, 36th Congress, first session, appendix, p. 367.
[2] *Globe, op. cit.*, p. 367.   [3] *Ibid.*, p. 295.
[4] 3 Wisconsin Reports, 1.

viewed and reversed by the Supreme Court of the United States in an opinion that established beyond question the superiority of national laws and the national administration over the states.[1]   Chief Justice Taney did not leave any doubt in the minds of the state officers that a national law, however obnoxious to local sentiment, must be upheld if need be by force of arms, and that a federal marshal must retain prisoners at all hazards regardless of the interference of state officers.   The opinion of the Chief Justice was in many respects, a stronger assertion of the right of judicial supremacy than any to be found in the opinions of Story or Marshall.   The position now maintained by Taney seems to contradict directly many of his former doctrines.

Rendering the opinion of the court, the Chief Justice noted that there were two cases.   In the first, a judge of the supreme court of Wisconsin claimed and exercised the right to annul the proceedings of a federal commissioner and to discharge a prisoner committed by him.   In the second, a state court claimed and exercised jurisdiction over the judgment of a district court of the United States and discharged a prisoner found guilty and imprisoned by this court.[2]   These decisions, the state affirmed, were final and conclusive over all federal courts.

The Chief Justice neglected to refer to the history of many former conflicts of a similar nature and claimed that for the first time the supremacy of state courts over the courts of the United States was asserted.   His reply was definite and decisive.   No state could authorize one of its judges or courts to exercise judicial power within the jurisdiction of another independent government.   Wisconsin was held to be sovereign only to the extent to which her

[1] 21 Howard, 506.   [2] *Ibid.*, 513, 514.

sovereignty was not limited by the Constitution of the
United States.[1] " And the sphere of action appropriated to
the United States is as far beyond the reach of judicial
process issued by a state judge, or a state court, as if the
line of division was traced by landmarks and monuments
visible to the eye." [2] The Supreme Court and the inferior
judicial tribunals of the federal government were spoken
of as the common arbiters between state and nation. Because of the danger of the influence of local interests the
final judicial power was placed in the Supreme Court of
the United States. The Chief Justice referred to the clause
of the Constitution which in his judgment had given the
Supreme Court jurisdiction over sovereign states. Ultimate appellate power in the Supreme Court was, he thought,
essential to secure the independence and supremacy of the
general government and from the decisions of this tribunal
there could be no appeal.[3] The fugitive-slave law was declared to be fully authorized by the Constitution and the
rights claimed by the state were emphatically denied.[4]

The state assembly, in March, 1859, resolved that " we
regard the action of the Supreme Court of the United
States in assuming jurisdiction . . as an act of arbitrary
power unauthorized by the Constitution, and virtually su-
perseding the benefit of the writ of *habeas corpus,* prostrat-
ing the rights and liberties of the people at the foot of unlimited power." [5] This assumption was accordingly denounced as an act of undelegated power, and declared to
be without authority, void, and of no force, and it was maintained that the government framed by the Constitution of
the United States was not made the exclusive or final judge
of the extent of the powers delegated to itself; and that

[1] 21 Howard, 515, 516.   [2] *Ibid.,* 516.   [3] *Ibid.,* 517-519.
[4] *Ibid.,* 526.   [5] Tyler, *Memoir of R. B. Taney,* p. 398.

" the principle and construction contended for by the party which now rules in the councils of the nation, . . . stop nothing short of despotism, since the discretion of those who administer the government, and not the Constitution, would be the measure of their powers." [1] After being arrested several times Booth was pardoned by President Buchanan, thus bringing to a close the last conflict over judicial powers before the beginning of hostilities in 1861.

Lincoln's inaugural address. The country was hastening into civil war; the days of peaceful discussion and calm deliberation had passed. A new party, pledged to do all in its power to restrain the spread of slavery, had elected its President, and the country awaited the decision of the southern states which had threatened to secede. One by one, beginning in December, the southern states passed secession ordinances while the United States government feebly tried to bring about a reconciliation. At the time of the inauguration of the new President practically the whole south was in a state of armed insurrection, while the national government had done almost nothing to meet an unprecedented state of affairs. President Lincoln knew that delay would be fatal. Prompt and decisive measures were necessary.

In his inaugural address the President indicated the attitude which the government under his administration would assume toward the Dred Scott decision as well as toward other instances of judicial interference in political affairs. The President announced a modified form of the Jacksonian doctrine:

I do not forget the position, assumed by some, that constitutional questions are to be decided by the Supreme Court; nor do I deny that such decisions must be binding, in any case,

[1] Tyler, *op. cit.*, p. 398.

upon the parties to a suit, as to the object of that suit, while they are also entitled to very high respect and consideration in all parallel cases by all other departments of the government. And while it is obviously possible that such decision may be erroneous in any given case, still the evil effect following it, being limited to that particular case, with the chance that it may be overruled and never become a precedent for other cases, can better be borne than could the evils of a different practice. At the same time, the candid citizen must confess that if the policy of the government, upon vital questions affecting the whole people, is to be irrevocably fixed by decisions of the Supreme Court, the instant they are made, in ordinary litigation between parties in personal actions, the people will have ceased to be their own rulers, having to that extent practically resigned their government into the hands of that eminent tribunal. Nor is there in this view, any assault upon the court or the judges. It is a duty from which they may not shrink to decide cases properly brought before them, and it is no fault of theirs if others seek to turn their decisions to political purposes.[1]

2. *Suspension of the writ of habeas corpus.*

Merryman case. An occasion soon arose in which the President was obliged to put into practice his theory regarding judicial authority. In order to render it possible to bring federal troops through the hostile state of Maryland the President suspended the writ of *habeas corpus.* On May 25th, 1861, John Merryman of Baltimore was arrested on the charge of acting in hostility to the government of the United States. He was lodged in Fort McHenry under the direction of General Cadwalader. On a petition to Chief Justice Taney for a writ of *habeas corpus* an order was granted May 27th, to which General Cadwalader failed to

[1] *Works,* vi, pp. 179-180.

respond, claiming that he was " duly authorized by the President of the United States to suspend the writ of *habeas corpus* for the public safety." [1]   May 27th, the Chief Justice issued a writ of attachment with the purpose of bringing the General before the court to answer for contempt in refusing to produce the body of Merryman.   On May 28th, the marshal informed the Chief Justice that he was not permitted to enter the fort and received no answer to the writ. [2]

The whole proceeding appeared to take the Chief Justice by surprise, with the result that he issued a hasty order and indicated that he would prepare an opinion to sustain his action.   In the oral statement justifying the order of the court Taney remarked that the President of the United States could not suspend the privilege of the writ of *habeas corpus* nor authorize a military officer to do so; and that a military officer had no right to arrest and detain a person not subject to the rules of war for an offence against the laws of the United States, except by judicial authority and subject to its control. [3]   Taney maintained that the marshal had the power to summon the *posse comitatus* to seize and bring into court the party named in the attachment; but as it was apparent that he would be resisted by a force notoriously superior to the *posse comitatus*, the court had no power under the law to order the necessary force to compel the appearance of the party. [4]

The Chief Justice later submitted a written opinion in which he charged that the President not only claimed the right to suspend the writ of *habeas corpus* himself, at his discretion, but to delegate that authority to a military officer and leave it to him to determine whether he would obey judicial process.   No official notice, Taney declared, had

[1] McPherson, *History of the Rebellion*, p. 154.   [2] *Ibid.*, p. 154.
[3] *Ibid.*, p. 155.   [4] *Ibid.*, p. 155.

been given that the President claimed this power or that he had exercised it in the manner indicated. He thought that it was admitted on all hands that the privilege of the writ of *habeas corpus* could not be suspended except by act of Congress.[1] After offering a carefully prepared argument in favor of the position assumed by the court, the Chief Justice concluded with the opinion that if such a state of affairs was permitted to exist " the people of the United States are no longer living under a government of laws, but every citizen holds life, liberty, and property at the will and pleasure of the army officers in whose military district he may happen to be found." [2]

In such a case Taney said " my duty was too plain to be mistaken. I have exercised all the power which the Constitution and laws confer on me, but that power has been resisted by a force too strong for me to overcome." With the possibility that the instructions might have been misunderstood, Taney ventured to turn the record of the whole proceeding over to the President with the reflection that it would then remain for him, in the fulfilment of his constitutional obligation to determine what measures he would take to uphold the judicial department of the government.[3]

In the meantime the President had submitted the question to his attorney-general, from whom he received the opinion that when a dangerous insurrection threatens the very existence of the nation, the President has the discretionary power to arrest and hold in custody " persons known to have criminal intercourse with the insurgents or persons against whom there is probable cause for suspicion of such criminal complicity," [4] and that the President has power to suspend the privilege of the writ of *habeas corpus* as to per-

---

[1] McPherson, *op. cit.*, p. 155.   [2] *Ibid.*, p. 158.
[3] *Ibid.*, p. 158.   [4] *Ibid.*, p. 159.

sons arrested under such circumstances, since he is especially charged by the Constitution with the preservation of the public safety and is the sole judge of the emergency which requires prompt action; and for any breach of trust he is responsible to the high court of impeachment but to no other tribunal.[1] Acting on this view, the order of General Cadwalader was upheld and the right of judicial interference denied. In a proclamation issued in February, 1862, President Lincoln referred to this incident when he said that " the judicial machinery seemed as if it had been designed not to sustain the government, but to embarrass and betray it." [2]

Prize cases. At the opening of the December term of court in 1861, the attorney-general informed the justices that their lawful jurisdiction was practically restrained, their just power diminished, and their beneficent authority to administer justice according to law was successfully denied and resisted in a large portion of the country.[3] It remained to be seen whether the judicial department would quietly acquiesce while the political departments of the government were waging the contest for the preservation of the Union. Several of the justices were known to be opposed to the methods of the President in the conduct of the war. When the Prize cases came before the Supreme Court in 1862, wherein the question was raised whether the President had a right to institute a blockade of ports in possession of persons in armed rebellion against the government,[4] there were apprehensions lest the judiciary might interfere with the course which the executive was pursuing. The court, however, by a majority of one, in an opinion based upon the principles of international law relating to belligerents, affirmed the policy of President Lincoln.

[1] McPherson, *op. cit.*, p. 161.   [2] *Works*, vii, p. 101.
[3] 1 Black, 9.   [4] 2 Black, 635.

Justice Grier, in delivering the opinion of the court, declared that it was not the less a civil war because it was called an insurrection by the one side, and the insurgents were considered as rebels or traitors.[1] Referring to the course of affairs thus far, he continued,

After such an official recognition by the sovereign, a citizen of a foreign state is estopped to deny the existence of a war with all its consequences as regards neutrals. They cannot ask a court to affect a technical ignorance of the existence of a war, which all the world acknowledges to be the greatest civil war known in the history of the human race, and thus cripple the arm of the government and paralyze its power by subtle definitions and ingenious sophisms. The law of nations is also called the law of nature; it is founded on the common consent, as well as the common sense of the world. It contains no such anomalous doctrines as that which this court is now for the first time desired to pronounce, to wit: that the insurgents who have risen in rebellion against their sovereign, expelled her courts, established a revolutionary government, organized armies, and commenced hostilities, are not enemies because they are traitors; and a war levied on the government by traitors, in order to dismember and destroy it, is not a war, because it is an insurrection.[2]

According to this opinion the character and nature of the resistance to be used against the insurrection had to be determined by the President, and the courts were of necessity obliged to recognize as final the decisions and acts of the political departments of the government.[3] The court regarded the contest as in the realm of war between nations, with all its attending consequences, and thus placed the national authorities in a much stronger position than would

[1] 2 Black, 669.   [2] *Ibid.*, 669.   [3] *Ibid.*, 669, 670.

otherwise have been possible. The judicial department realized the necessity of upholding the military authorities, and appreciated the fact that most of the questions arising out of the state of warfare did not belong to the realm of duties allotted to courts of justice. A dissenting opinion was offered by Justice Nelson and was concurred in by Chief Justice Taney, Justices Catron and Clifford. After a graphic description of the nature of the state of war, Justice Nelson declared that by our Constitution the power to bring about such a condition is lodged in Congress.[1] In order that a war may legally exist it must be recognized or declared by the war-making power of the government. No power short of this could change the legal status of the government or the relations of its citizens from that of peace to a state of war.[2] Accordingly the conduct of affairs during the first period of the rebellion was designated as a personal war, and it was claimed that the actual state of war did not come into existence until after the act of Congress on the 13th of July, 1861, went into effect.[3] In short, the President had no right to declare war nor did he possess the constitutional power to institute a blockade.

Case of Vallandigham. Among the many democrats who were inclined to denounce the republican administration, especially in its conduct of the war, was Vallandigham, a politician in the state of Ohio. Vallandigham was a candidate for the democratic nomination for governor at the time General Burnside was assigned to the command of the department of Ohio. On April 13th, the General issued an order decreeing the penalty of death upon all those who were in the habit of declaring sympathy for the enemy.[4] For some radical remarks at a democratic mass meeting on

---

[1] 2 Black, 688.   [2] *Ibid.*, 689.   [3] *Ibid.*, 694, 695.
[4] For history of this case see Rhodes, *op. cit.*, iv, pp. 246-255.

May 1st, Vallandigham was arrested under the General's order and thrown into a military prison. After a mere form of a trial which resulted in a sentence for detention until the end of the war, an attempt was made to bring the matter to a close by sending the prisoner over to the confederacy. The whole proceeding was an extreme assertion of military authority and caused considerable difficulty for the administration.[1]

The Supreme Court, in an appeal which was brought to free Vallandigham did not feel inclined to interfere, although the arrest was made under circumstances similar to those which led the court later to deny this authority to the executive. Regardless of the fact that the General's order was issued with full knowledge that there was an act of Congress covering the case, four members of the Supreme Court concurred in the opinion that the court had no power to review the proceedings of a military commission ordered by a general of the United States.[2]

The greatest difficulty, however, arose on account of the criticisms of the party press. Resolutions of condemnation were frequently forwarded to President Lincoln. The tenor of these criticisms is shown in a summary of one series of resolutions when a political gathering in Ohio inquired whether he really claimed that he might override all the guaranteed rights of individuals, on the plea of conserving the public safety, whenever he chose to say the public safety required it.[3]

Although Lincoln confessed that he regretted the necessity of arresting Vallandigham, and doubted whether he would have ordered his arrest, nevertheless he decided to assume the responsibility for the whole proceeding.

---

[1] Rhodes, p. 248.   [2] 1 Wallace, 385.
[3] *Works*, vol. ix, pp. 3, 4.

In a letter to Erastus Corning relative to a series of resolutions at a public meeting in Albany, Lincoln wrote: " the meeting by their resolutions, assert and argue that certain military arrests and proceedings following them for which I am ultimately responsible, are unconstitutional. I think they are not." [1] They claimed that the arrest of Vallandigham was made for no other reason than for words addressed to a public meeting in criticism of the course of the administration, and in condemnation of the military orders of a general. Though Vallandigham's conduct was not strictly within the law of Congress, Lincoln regarded it as resistance to the military, which under the state of affairs at the time, could not be permitted. [2]

Yet, thoroughly imbued with a reverence for the guaranteed rights of individuals, I was slow to adopt the strong measures which by degrees I have been forced to regard as being within the exceptions of the Constitution, and as indispensable to the public safety. Nothing is better known to history than that courts of justice are utterly incompetent to such cases . . . a jury too frequently has at least one member more ready to hang the panel than to hang the traitor. And yet again, he who dissuades one man from volunteering or induces one soldier to desert, weakens the Union cause as much as he who kills a Union soldier in battle. [3]

The letter was closed with the warning that, although the President was sorry Vallandigham had to be arrested, he must continue to do whatever might seem to be required by the public safety. [4]

Milligan case. When the war was brought to a successful conclusion the Supreme Court felt at liberty to deliver

---

[1] *Works*, vol. viii, p. 299.   [2] *Ibid.*, pp. 307, 308.
[3] *Ibid.*, vol. viii, pp. 303, 304.   [4] *Ibid.*, vol. viii, p. 314.

an opinion in line with the sentiments of its members.[1] It was then announced by Justice Davis for the court that the federal authority, having been unopposed in the state of Indiana, and the federal courts open for the trial of offences and redress of grievances, the usages of war could not under the Constitution afford any sanction for the trial of a citizen in civil life by a military tribunal for any offence whatever.[2] Although the proceedings were known to have had the fullest sanction of the executive department of the government, the judgment was rendered without a dissenting voice. Several members of the court, however, took exception to the extreme position of Justice Davis, when he insisted that neither Congress nor the President had the power to authorize a military commission to proceed to trial and judgment under the conditions which existed in Indiana. Justice Davis maintained that " martial rule can never exist where the courts are open, and in the proper and unobstructed exercise of their jurisdiction." [3] Four members of the court declined to go so far, and held instead that Congress had the power to establish such a military commission as that which was held in Indiana.[4] A few decisions which followed in quick succession merely tended to arouse Congress to such an extent that the appellate jurisdiction of the federal courts was restricted.

3. The attitude of the Supreme Court toward Reconstruction

The test oath cases. Immediately after the close of the Civil War stringent laws were passed against those who had taken part in the rebellion. A provision of the constitution of Missouri, adopted in 1865, prescribed an oath to be taken by all officers, teachers, preachers, and all those serving in any public capacity, or by anyone desiring to participate in

---

[1] 4 Wallace, 2.   [2] *Ibid.*, 126, 127.
[3] *Ibid.*, 127.   [4] *Ibid.*, 137.

the election of such officers.[1] The oath was directed against all those who had assisted in the rebellion, and practically disqualified any person who had manifested in the least his adherence to the cause of the enemies of the United States. There was a severe penalty for continuing in public service without taking the oath. Under the authority of this provision, Cummings, a catholic priest, was sentenced to pay a fine of five hundred dollars and to be committed to jail until said fine and costs were paid. The supreme court of Missouri affirmed the judgment and the case was brought into the courts of the United States on a writ of error.[2]

About the same time Congress prescribed a similar oath for all attorneys and counselors desiring to appear before the courts of the United States. Garland, who had been admitted to practice before the Supreme Court previous to the war, participated in the rebellion and then returned and demanded admission without taking the oath prescribed by Congress and administered by the court.[3] The counsel contended that the provision of the constitution of Missouri and the law of Congress were contrary to the Constitution of the United States, both as bills of attainder and as ex post facto laws. The court held that under the form of creating a qualification or attaching a condition, the states could not in effect inflict a punishment for a past act which was not punishable at the time it was committed.[4] The provision of the constitution of Missouri and the law of Congress instead of requiring a qualification relative to the duties of the office imposed a punishment for past conduct. Although the prohibition of ex post facto laws was aimed at criminal cases, it could not be evaded by giving a civil form to that which was in substance criminal. As a result of the prin-

---

[1] Cummings *vs.* Missouri, 4 Wallace, 279-281.

[2] *Ibid.*, 281, 282.   [3] 4 Wallace, 335-337.   [4] *Ibid.*, 319.

ciples thus announced, the court held that the provision of the Constitution and the law of Congress were both bills of attainder and ex post facto laws, and as such had to be considered null and void.

There was a strong dissenting opinion by Justice Miller concurred in by the Chief Justice and two associate justices, which applied to both cases. Referring to the English bills of attainder it was claimed that " a statute, then, which designates no criminal, either by name or description—which declares no guilt, pronounces no sentence, and inflicts no punishment—can in no sense be called a bill of attainder." [1] As to ex post facto laws, " all the cases agree that the term is to be applied to criminal cases alone, and not to civil proceedings." [2] The dissenting justices could see nothing in the nature of a punishment in the oaths required. They held that Congress had the right to prescribe the oath as a qualification for all those who wished to take part in the administration of the government, and that the state, in the exercise of its exclusive power over the subject of religion, could so control public morals and public order as to exclude all those from preaching or teaching who had shown any disposition to oppose the government of the United States. [3]

Up to the time of the test oath cases the Supreme Court was not at all inclined to apply the clause in the Constitution prohibiting bills of attainder and ex post facto laws to the protection of the individual in the realm of civil rights. [4] Justice Miller in his dissent, which applied to both cases,

[1] 4 Wallace, 390.   [2] Ibid., 390.   [3] Ibid., 396-399.
[4] See Watson vs. Mercer, wherein it was held that " ex post facto laws relate to penal and criminal proceedings which impose punishments or forfeitures, and not to civil proceedings which effect private rights retrospectively." 8 Peters, 110.

commented as follows: " the act which has just been declared to be unconstitutional is nothing more than a statute which requires of all lawyers who propose to practice in the national courts, that they shall take the same oath which is exacted of every officer of the government civil or military." [1] The opinion of the majority was condemned inferentially by Justice Miller in the remark that " I have endeavored to bring to the examination of the great questions of constitutional law involved in this inquiry those principles alone which are calculated to assist in determining what the law is, rather than what, in my judgment, it ought to be." [2]

When Congress indicated its intention to pursue radical measures toward the reconstruction of the governments of the southern states, regardless of the objections of President Johnson, several southern states attempted to prevent the execution of these acts by appealing to the Supreme Court. Mississippi filed a bill in equity asking the Supreme Court to enjoin Andrew Johnson perpetually from executing certain reconstruction acts. [3] Georgia also filed a bill to enjoin the enforcement of these laws. [4] Both appeals were denied on the ground that the bills required the interference of the court in a political issue which was plainly contrary to previous practice. Though the acts of the President and Congress were admitted to be subject to the cognizance of the Supreme Court in proper cases, these were not regarded as cases for judicial interference.

The case of McCardle. It was feared that the excitement over reconstruction would be increased by interference

---

[1] 4 Wallace, 385.   [2] *Ibid.*, 399.
[3] The State of Mississippi *vs.* Andrew Johnson, *ibid.*, 475.
[4] The State of Georgia *vs.* Stanton, 6 Wallace, 50.

on the part of the Supreme Court. Five of the nine justices were known to be opposed to the congressional policy
of reconstruction. The arrest of McCardle by a military
commission in Mississippi under the provisions of one of
these acts led to an appeal to the Supreme Court. The first
question raised was with regard to jurisdiction, which was
decided in favor of the Supreme Court in an opinion by
Chief Justice Chase. The Chief Justice claimed that prior
to the passage of the act of 1867 appellate jurisdiction was
exercised over the action of inferior courts by *habeas corpus*.
As this authority had not been removed no doubt was entertained that an appeal might be taken from the judgment
of the circuit court to the Supreme Court.[1]

Alarmed at the dangers of an adverse decision, and determined to admit of no interference, Congress passed an
act which practically took away jurisdiction over the Mc-
Cardle case.[2] It was then argued that the act of Congress
was a manifest assault upon the judicial department of the
government and therefore unconstitutional. The act was
thought to be equivalent to the doctrine that the Supreme
Court should never give judgment in any case contrary to
the views of the majority in Congress.[3] When the case was
again presented Chief Justice Chase held that the court was
not at liberty to inquire into the motives of the legislature.
The court originally had been granted jurisdiction, and now
that by act of Congress this jurisdiction had been taken
away, it was quite clear that the court could not proceed
to pronounce judgment in this case.[4] The sentiment in
Congress relative to the exercise of the right of declaring
legislative acts void was aroused to such an extent that this

[1] 6 Wallace, 324.

[2] *United States Statutes at Large*, xv, p. 44, March 27, 1868.

[3] 7 Wallace, 510.   [4] *Ibid.*, 515.

decision was the only one which could have avoided a serious contest between the two departments. The opinions of a few members of Congress indicate the tendency of the time to disregard judicial decisions.

Radical doctrines in Congress. In the session of Congress after the decision had been rendered in the Milligan case, in the consideration of a reconstruction bill, Thaddeus Stevens severely criticised the attitude of the Supreme Court. The late decision of the Supreme Court of the United States, he maintained, had rendered absolutely indispensable immediate action by Congress upon the question of the establishment of governments in the rebel states. " That decision, although in terms not as infamous as the Dred Scott decision, is yet far more dangerous in its operations upon the lives and liberties of the loyal men of this country." [1] One member reminded the house that those desiring clemency might appeal to the Supreme Court for such protection as a majority of that body were inclined to grant to rebels, and begged the house to commit itself to no such folly.[2] But in discussing the possibility of interference from the Supreme Court, he remarked, " the court should recollect that it has had bad luck with its political decisions. The people of this country thus far have preferred to govern the country themselves and let the court attend to its law business. Both of its great political opinions had been overruled by an appeal to the ballot-box.[3]

In the discussion of a proposed amendment to the Constitution another member took occasion to deliver a harangue against the court and the executive, when told that the Supreme Court of the United States would strike down the

---

[1] *Congressional Globe,* 39th Congress, second session, p. 251, January 3, 1867.

[2] *Ibid.,* p. 255.   [3] *Ibid.,* p. 255.

amendment. That supreme tribunal of justice, he thought, had no power to give a decision, for it was a political question in which a court could in no way interfere. The decision of Congress, he declared, was final and conclusive over every judicial tribunal in the land. Neither the executive nor the judicial departments had any voice in the matter: any right to challenge the authority of the people.[1]

On January 21st, 1867, a bill was introduced requiring a unanimous decision by the court on questions involving the constitutionality of laws.[2] And on January 13th, 1868, a similar bill came up for consideration. Williams of Pennsylvania noted that there was a case now pending in the Supreme Court of the United States which demanded immediate action by the House. Such a decision he thought would simply awaken both houses to the necessity of defending the legislative power which is the true sovereign of the nation.[3] On the issue whether decisions on questions of constitutionality ought to be given by a unanimous opinion or by a two-thirds majority, Mr. Williams argued that a dissent implies a doubt and most lawyers would agree that in cases where there is a dissent among the members of the court, the opinion of the dissenting judges would almost invariably be found to be the better one.[4]

Sometime earlier a bill had been offered for the purpose of providing that certain persons should not hold the office of attorney or counselor in any court of the United States. This bill was presented in direct opposition to the decision of the Supreme Court. It was believed that if the judges of the highest tribunal would not by proper regulations protect themselves from the contamination of conspirators and traitors against the government, the time had arrived when

---

[1] *Globe,* pp. 501, 502, January 16, 1867.

[2] *Ibid.,* p. 616.   [3] *Ibid.,* p. 478.   [4] *Ibid.,* p. 479.

the legislative department should exercise its power to declare who should be admitted to practice in the courts of the Union.[1]   In reply it was argued that such a law would be a palpable and manifest usurpation of the powers delegated to the great conservative department of the government.[2]

On the consideration of a supplementary reconstruction bill, on January 28, 1868, it was claimed that the idea which had gone forth, that the judiciary could render a decision on the subject of reconstruction, was a strange one.   The members of Congress did not suppose that it was intended for one or five members of the Supreme Court to regulate the political interests and relations of the country.   It was said that if the Supreme Court would decide the reconstruction acts unconstitutional, the moral effect would be injurious; and if the Supreme Court would deliberately usurp the authority of the legislature, Congress had the right to withdraw all supervisory power over the reconstructions acts.[3]

The expression of such radical opinions in Congress, together with the act passed over the President's veto removing the McCardle case from the jurisdiction of the court, was sufficient warning that Congress would allow no interference in the program which had been planned.   The legislature hereafter dealt with a free hand in the districts where the reconstruction acts applied.   Congress had "subdued the Supreme Court "[4] and brought it to a realization of the fact that the state of war had not fully passed away, and that the old-time co-ordination of departments with the Supreme Court as final interpreter could not be tolerated in dealing

[1] *Globe,* January 22, 1867, pp. 646, 647.
[2] *Ibid.,* p. 488.   [3] *Ibid.,* p. 791.
[4] *Memoirs of B. R. Curtis,* vol. i, p. 421.

with the states of the confederacy.   The court had to suffer one more reversal in the series of conflicts beginning in 1856 before affairs began to settle back to the peaceful condition which had prevailed before the war.

4. *Legal Tender Cases.*

In order to meet the exigencies of the war the national government had enacted two laws which made United States notes legal tender in the payment of all debts, public and private.   These statutes had been the law of the land for a period of almost seven years when they were assailed before the Supreme Court on the charge of unconstitutionality.[1]

It was confidently expected in many quarters that the experience of the court, in the disrespect shown to former decisions wherein the acts of the other departments were challenged, would serve as a warning against future interference with congressional legislation.   The majority of the court, however, were of the opinion that there was in the Constitution no express grant of legislative authority to make any description of credit currency a legal tender in payment of debts contracted before the passage of the acts of 1862 and 1863 and that these acts were inconsistent with the spirit of the Constitution, and therefore prohibited by it.[2]   The opinion was closed with the declaration, " we are obliged to conclude that an act making mere promises to pay dollars a legal tender in payment of debts previously contracted, is not a means appropriate, plainly adapted, really calculated to carry into effect any express power vested in Congress; and that such an act is inconsistent with the spirit of the Constitution; and that it is prohibited

[1] 8 Wallace, 603.   [2] *Ibid.*, 623, 624.

by the Constitution." [1]   The Chief Justice who rendered the opinion then took occasion to state the reasons for his change of attitude from the time when, as secretary of the treasury, he had favored this form of legislation.

The decision indicated that the court was inclined to insist that the interpretation of the Constitution by the court on the financial policy of the government was superior to that of Congress and the President.   Three justices dissented with the remark that such an opinion of the court, annulling the law after years of general acceptance, substituted the court's ideas of policy for judicial construction and an indefinite code of ethics for the national legislature. [2]

The steps which led to a reconsideration and reversal of this deliberate opinion of the court furnished an instance where political influence may fairly be assumed to have determined a judicial decision.   Four justices in the first case, all democrats in their political way of thinking, held that these laws were unconstitutional.   Three republican members concurred in the dissenting opinion, thereby upholding the acts of a republican administration.   Under an act of Congress increasing the number of justices, which had been passed sometime before the decision was announced, two republicans were appointed, both known to favor the constitutionality of the laws; and the same question was again brought up for argument.   This time by a majority of one, the acts were declared constitutional and the former decision overruled. [3]   The fact that Justice Grier first favored the constitutionality of the acts and then changed his opinion, making a majority against the laws, and that he was later asked to resign because of his conduct in this case, did not tend to dispel the suspicion that the reargument after the

[1] 8 Wallace, 625.   [2] *Ibid.*, 638.
[3] Legal Tender cases, 12 Wallace, 457.

appointment of new justices was another attempt to bring the judicial department in subjection to the political tendencies of the time.

The conflicts over judicial powers growing out of the struggle between the North and the South were brought to a close in this series of decisions. The ascendency of the executive department during the time of warfare, followed by the supremacy of the legislative department in the period of reconstruction, was replaced by a condition in which the courts gradually assumed an even stronger position than had been possible in any previous period.

As a result of the principles of the Jacksonian democracy, the loss of prestige on account of the Dred Scott decision, the complete subordination of judicial authority during the war and the notable reverses in the attempt to interfere with reconstruction, it might seem that the authority of the courts was on the decline. From all appearances the practice of declaring legislative acts void was losing its importance as a permanent feature of the the national government.

A study· of the development of judicial authority since 1870 will, however, dispel any idea as to the weakening of the powers of the courts in the United States. The Supreme Court and all inferior judicial tribunals in the country are not only restored to their former place of influence and power, but are once more recognized as the final interpreters of constitutions and laws. At the same time the courts have been inevitably drawn into the social and economic conflicts arising in the course of our rapid industrial development, and there is an increasing number of instances in which judicial authority is being challenged in such a manner as to make it again the subject of political controversy.

VITA

THE writer of this essay was born in Lineboro, Maryland, September 20th, 1879. His elementary education was completed at the East Berlin high school, Adams County, Penna., and his college preparatory work, at Eichelberg Academy, Hanover, Penna., from which he was graduated in June, 1899. September, 1899, he entered Ursinus College and received therefrom the degree of Bachelor of Arts in June, 1903. The following three years were spent in the School of Political Science of Columbia University; 1903-4 as University Scholar in Constitutional Law and 1904-6, George William Curtis Fellow in Political Science. He attended the courses of Professors Burgess, Goodnow, Robinson, Moore, Dunning and Seligman, and the seminar of Professor Burgess. In June, 1904, he received the degree Master of Arts from Columbia University. The thesis submitted for the degree was on "Bills of Attainder and Ex Post Facto Laws." June, 1905, he was elected Professor of History and Political Science in Ursinus College where he has served as instructor since September, 1906.